Overcoming Age Discrimination in Employment

An Essential Guide for Workers,
Advocates & Employers

Patricia G. Barnes, J.D.

The past 50 years have seen a great revolution in the United States. Computers. Robots on assembly lines. Self-driving cars. The explosion of the Internet. But the Age Discrimination in Employment Act has not changed appreciably in a half century. Older workers literally have been second-class citizens under the law since the ADEA was adopted in 1967. This book is dedicated to the on-going struggle of older workers for respect, dignity and equal justice in the workplace.

Table of Contents

1. THIS IS GETTING OLD

"Discrimination due to age is one of the great tragedies of modern life. The desire to work and be useful is what makes life worth living, and to be told your efforts are not needed because you are the wrong age is a crime." – *Johnny Ball, the father of BBC Radio.*

The Age Discrimination in Employment Act (ADEA) is about to turn 50, a milestone of dubious distinction given the poor performance of the law. Congress enacted the ADEA in 1967 "to promote employment of older persons based on their ability rather than age; to prohibit arbitrary age discrimination in employment." However, the ADEA was weak and riddled with loopholes as adopted when compared to Title VII of the Civil Rights Act of 1964, which prohibits discrimination on the basis of race, sex, religion, color and national origin. Things have gone downhill for the ADEA ever since.

Age discrimination in employment is treated like a lesser offense in the United States.

Age discrimination is so prevalent today that it is almost invisible. For example, employers for years have posted internet and print job advertisements that are thinly disguised recruitments for workers under the age of 40 (i.e., "digital natives," "recent" college graduates). The ADEA prohibits publishing any advertisement that indicates a preference for applicants on the basis on age. If, instead of age, these advertisements sought male applicants of Scandinavian descent, the outcry would be immediate and widespread. Not so for age discrimination.

Age discrimination is so pervasive that it is considered normal in American society.

The normalization of age discrimination has caused a trickle-down effect. It is estimated that about 75 percent of workers who file age discrimination lawsuits are under the age of 60. In some industries, age discrimination impacts workers who are not yet middle-aged!

An age discrimination lawsuit filed against Google, the search engine giant, revealed that the median age of Google's 28,000 employees in 2013 was 29. Statistics from the U.S. Dept. of Labor show this is well below the median age of 42.8 for computer programmers and 40.6 for software developers in the United States.

My earlier book, BETRAYED: THE LEGALIZATION OF AGE DISCRIMINATION IN THE WORKPLACE (2014), indisputably shows that victims of age discrimination are second-class citizens under U.S. law. I urge Congress to scrap the ADEA and make age a protected class under Title VII, as was originally proposed fifty years ago. This would at least insure that older workers have equal rights. It is not a revolutionary step; Australia did the equivalent of this in 2009 to insure equality for older workers.

OVERCOMING AGE DISCRIMINATION IN EMPLOYMENT shows victims of age discrimination and their advocates how to:

- Identify illegal age discrimination in employment.
- File a complaint with the U.S. Equal Employment Opportunity Commission.
- Use the law to overcome age discrimination and hold employers to account.

> **This book explains:**
> - **Age discrimination in employment;**
> - **When it is illegal; and,**
> - **How to respond to and overcome the problem.**

This book also is a valuable resource for employers and human resource departments because it explains how the ADEA works in the real world. Smart employers avoid age discrimination because it creates potential risk and alienates or drives out valuable workers of all ages. At some point, even younger workers think twice about committing their future to a workplace where they can see there is no future.

Citations are provided for readers who wish to take the next step and research key cases and studies. Everyone else can ignore them.

Given the aging population in the U.S., it is surprising how little attention is paid to the problem of age discrimination in employment. One reason is that there is no equivalent of an organization like the NAACP or National Organization for Women demanding equal rights for older workers. For whatever reason, the AARP, which purports to advocate for Americans aged 50 and over, has had little impact on the systemic problem of age discrimination in employment.

Many older workers don't realize how few rights they have until they experience age discrimination. Then they discover that it is hard to find an attorney who doesn't demand a five-figure advance (or more). If they proceed without an attorney, their case may be summarily dismissed prior to trial by a federal judge because of some obscure technicality. Too often, the problem of age discrimination sinks into a quicksand of chronic unemployment, under-employment and, finally, forced retirement.

Because there is so little help out there, it is imperative that all workers understand and recognize age discrimination. It almost always better to confront the problem as soon as possible. The consequences of age discrimination in employment can be severe and irreversible. Most age discrimination cases involve job loss and once older workers lose their job, it can be extremely difficult to find equivalent new employment.

Age discrimination forces many older workers into a financially ill-advised early retirement. The Social Security Administration effectively penalizes age discrimination victims who are forced to retire at age 62. The SSA's benefit formula automatically reduces the monthly benefit of individuals who retire at age 62 by *at least* 25 percent for the rest of their lives compared to workers who retire at age 66. Not surprisingly, age discrimination in employment is correlated with elder poverty.

Sixty-three percent of age discrimination complaints filed with the EEOC involve the loss of a job.

There is overwhelming evidence that age discrimination is epidemic and unaddressed in America. An AARP survey in

2015 found that half of people aged 45 to 70 who had experienced unemployment during the past five years were either still unemployed or had dropped out of the labor force.[1] Of those who were working, nearly half said they were earning less than in their previous jobs.

The Perfect Storm

Age discrimination is and has always been deeply ingrained in the human psyche, grounded in fears of decline, ill health and death. And it has always been regarded by the American legal system as less worthy of protection than other types of employment discrimination. But something is clearly different today. Economic upheavals and the disappearance of traditional pensions have changed the scale and impact of the problem. A confluence of circumstances have made the problem of age discrimination in employment more severe today than in our parents' generation.

Age discrimination complaints skyrocketed during the Great Recession.

First, the Great Recession was a crippling blow for millions of older workers. The EEOC received 24,582 age discrimination complaints in 2008 - an increase of 29 percent

[1] *Half of Older Workers Who Were Unemployed in Last Five Years Jobless today, According to AARP Survey*, March 20, 2015, viewed on 12/10/15 at http://www.aarp.org/about-aarp/press-center/info-03-2015/older-workers-unemployment-survey.html

over 2007 and the highest number in the EEOC's history. 2008. And this was a drop in a very large bucket. The EEOC's response was disappointing and continues to be. The level of complaints remains elevated compared with pre-recession levels but the number of EEOC lawsuits with age discrimination claims has declined from 38 in 2008 to seven in 2013 and twelve in 2014. The EEOC has ignored the increase in age discrimination complaints. To be fair, federal courts have been hostile to age discrimination complainants (and the EEOC) in recent years.

Meanwhile, the U.S. Supreme Court has made it inordinately difficult for age discrimination plaintiffs to prevail in federal courts. The Court in 2009 required ADEA plaintiffs to prove a much higher standard of causation than is required under Title VII.[2] A proposed law to fix this disastrous ruling - the Protecting Older Workers Against Discrimination Act – has been mired in Congressional subcommittees for six years and counting.

The U.S. Supreme Court accords age discrimination less protection than discrimination on the basis of race, sex, religion, color and national origin.

The Supreme Court historically has accorded age discrimination the lowest of its three tiers of protection. A

---

[2] *Gross v. FBL Financial Services, Inc.*, 557 U.S. 167 (2009).

law that discriminates on the basis of age literally has to be irrational to offend the Court. It is accorded the Court's lowest level of scrutiny. By comparison, the Court uses its highest level of scrutiny - exacting "strict scrutiny" - for racially discriminatory laws. The Court uses either "strict" or "intermediate" scrutiny for laws that discriminate on the basis of sex. It is inherently contradictory for a court that was created under the U.S. Constitution to insure equal justice for all to deny equal justice to older workers.

State court judges in several states have filed federal lawsuits in recent years to overturn state laws requiring them to retire at age 70. All of these cases were dismissed under the "rational basis" standard of review. As he lowered the gavel on one case, a federal judge expressed discomfort, noting that he has lifetime tenure and never has to retire.

Legitimizing Age Discrimination

Another reason that age discrimination is worse today is that it has been bestowed with a kind of perverse legitimization. It is justified as a means to increase "diversity" in employment for young minority workers.

President Barack H. Obama signed an executive order in 2010 that permits the U.S. Office of Personnel Management (OPM) to discriminate against older workers by limiting hiring at federal agencies to "recent graduates." This runs contrary to decades of federal policy encouraging minority and youth hiring through educational and training programs.

Obama said he wanted to remove "barriers" to hiring younger workers caused by civil service regulations and "to achieve a workforce that represents all segments of society." Obama's policy makes age and experience, which is highly correlated with age, disqualifying characteristics for federal employment. He also said he wanted to "infuse" the federal government with the "enthusiasm, talents and unique perspective" of young people. This comment reflects ageist stereotypes that older workers are depressed, used up, and behind the times. Both sides of this equation are untrue – young people don't necessarily have enthusiasm, talent and a unique perspective. Older workers don'ts necessarily lack these traits. Ironically, civil service regulations were adopted in the late 1800s to insure fairness in hiring and to remove political cronyism.

Not only is the federal government is the nation's largest employer but Obama's executive order sent an unfortunate message to private sector employers– it's okay to ignore the ADEA and engage in age discrimination in employment.

> *Obama essentially justified age discrimination as a means to combat other forms of employment discrimination.*

If that wasn't bad enough, Obama's Labor Secretary, Thomas E. Perez, publicly endorsed a private 2015 initiative by some of America's leading corporations to hire 100,000 inner city residents between the ages of 16 and 24 for full-time and part-time jobs. The ADEA expressly prohibits age-based hiring in all but a few limited circumstances that do not apply here. Perez' endorsement of illegal age discrimination by corporations like Microsoft and Starbucks appears to be based upon an unsupported theory that disadvantaged young minority group members are more deserving than disadvantaged older minority group members (not to mention everyone else).

There are many problems with Obama's winners/losers approach. It is fundamentally contrary to basic American values to favor some discrimination victims over others. It arguably violates the Equal Protection Clause of the U.S. Constitution to single out older workers to receive lesser protection under federal law. And it is counterproductive and short-sighted. Discrimination cannot be contained in neat little categories. Age discrimination builds on race and sex discrimination. The cumulative effect of all employment discrimination explains why women and minorities suffer the highest rates of poverty in their old age. By encouraging age discrimination, Obama has merely kicked the problem of race discrimination down the road. There is no denying that youth unemployment is a major problem and that greater diversity is highly desirable in federal government but the solution is not to discriminate against older workers. Why not, for example, eliminate government policies that encourage unprecedented wealth inequality and which force all protected groups to compete with each other for the equivalent of stale crumbs.

Better Tools to Discriminate

Age discrimination appears to be far more damaging to older workers today because employers have much more effective tools at their disposal to discriminate against older workers. For years now, legions of older workers have told the same story about sending out hundreds of resumes without getting any response. The evidence is mounting that governmental and private sector employers are using computer programs to screen out the applications of older workers.

Employers have better tools to discriminate in the Internet age.

An EEOC investigation disclosed that R.J. Reynolds Tobacco, Co. worked with two international recruiting firms, Kelly Services and Pinstripe, from 2007 to 2010 to use the internet to screen applications for the position of regional sales manager. Reynolds and the recruiting firms agreed to the following "screening" criteria:

"...desired characteristics of the 'targeted candidate,' including '2-3 years out of college,' and characteristics of candidates to 'stay away from,' including applicants who were 'in sales for 8-10 years.'"

Reynolds hired 1,024 people from September 1, 2007 to July 10, 2010 to fill the regional sales manager positions. Of those, only 19 or 1.85 percent were over the age of 40.

Despite overwhelming evidence of age discrimination, a federal judge granted Reynold's pre-trial motion to dismiss an age discrimination lawsuit filed by an older applicants who was not hired. Bucking a national trend, an appeals court in 2015 reversed the dismissal and reinstated the case.[3] A conflict now exists in the federal circuits as to whether job applicants can file age discrimination lawsuits. This conflict can only be resolved by the U.S. Supreme Court.

Even great employees in a thriving economy have no right to keep their job.

Even in the best of circumstances, such as when the government demands that employers obey the law, it is not difficult for employers to hide age discrimination. An obscure 18th century legal doctrine called the "employment at will"

---

[3] See *Villarreal v. R.J. Reynolds Tobacco Company, Pinstripe, Inc. CareerBuilder, LLC.*, No. 15-10602 (11th Cir., Nov. 30, 2015).

rule allows employers to fire a worker for any reason or no reason at all. The only limitation is that employers cannot violate a law (i.e. Title VII, whistleblower protection) or narrowly-defined public policy. Age discrimination frequently lurks behind subjective language contained in a "poor performance" review.

Moreover, bogus layoffs are a favorite vehicle for age discrimination. During the Great Recession, older workers were shed from company payrolls like rain from an umbrella. Many employers used layoffs to cut costs under the guise of a company "reorganization" or "restructuring." The Bureau of Labor Statistics reports the unemployment rate for adults 55 and over increased by 106 percent between 2008 and 2009, compared to 70 percent for the general population. Some unscrupulous employers had no need to cut costs but seized the opportunity created by economic chaos to replace older workers with lower-paid younger workers.

More Vulnerable

Another factor has made older workers more vulnerable to discrimination for a half century – it is the very law that was enacted to protect them. The ADEA permits far more discrimination than does Title VII of the Civil Rights Act. And a finding of age discrimination is less costly to employers than other types of discrimination. The ADEA (unlike Title

VII) does not permit plaintiffs to recover damages for emotional distress or punitive damages. In this way, the ADEA permits employers to engage in more discrimination with less risk.

Congress initially considered adding age as a protected class to Title VII in 1964 but supposedly decided more study was needed on the problem of age discrimination. When the ADEA was passed in 1967, it reflected three years of intense lobbying by business interests. The ADEA was weak and riddled with loopholes when compared to Title VII.

By then, the EEOC was deluged with Title VII civil rights complaints so Congress assigned the U.S. Department of Labor (DOL) the task of enforcing the ADEA. To make it easier for the DOL, Congress patterned the damages section of the ADEA after that of the other major law enforced by DOL, the Fair Labor Standards Act (FLSA), which governs the payment of wages and overtime.

The ADEA's damages provisions are not generous because age discrimination is treated like a failure to pay overtime. This, in turn, lessens the deterrent effect of the ADEA.

All of these failures and omissions have had a huge of impact on the prevalence of age discrimination in the United States. In a 2013 survey, about one in six workers told the AARP that they were treated worse by their employer because of their age - which is at least double the comparable figure for those who said they are treated worse because of their education, gender, race, ethnicity, sexual orientation or religion.[4] More than 92 percent of those polled said age discrimination in the workplace is common or somewhat common.[5]

No justification exists for treating age discrimination less severely than other types of employment discrimination.

Society's greater tolerance for age discrimination stands in sharp contrast to a fundamental truth. There is inherently no substantive difference between age discrimination and any other type of irrational and damaging discrimination. If older workers are incapable of performing the duties of a job, they should be fired just like anyone else. Discrimination occurs when workers who are adequately performing a job are

---

[4] AARP, *Staying Ahead of the Curve 2013: The AARP Work and Career Study. Older Workers in an Uneasy Job Market*, p. 9 (January 2014), retrieved on 7/15/15 from
http://www.aarp.org/content/dam/aarp/research/surveys_statistics/gen eral/2014/Staying-Ahead-of-the-Curve-2013-The-Work-and-Career-Study-AARP-res-gen.pdf
[5] *Staying Ahead of the Curve 2013: AARP Multicultural Work and Career Study Perceptions of Age Discrimination in the Workplace* – Ages 45-74. Downloaded on 9/16/15 from:
http://www.aarp.org/content/dam/aarp/research/surveys_statistics/eco n/2013/Staying-Ahead-of-the-Curve-Age-Discrimination.pdf

subjected to an adverse employment action because of their age.

Age discrimination in employment is an outgrowth of pervasive ageism in American society. Just as in race or sex discrimination, older people are targets of fear, animus and false stereotypes. In this case, it is fear of mortality and death. Moreover, they are widely depicted as incontinent, constipated, impotent, unhealthy, depressed, depressing, senile, helpless, greedy, cranky, and, most of all, uncool. One of the worst aspects of ageism and ageist stereotypes is that older people internalize these negative messages and feel themselves less worthy of dignity, respect and fair treatment.

Let Them Eat Cake?

One of the stereotypes used to justify age discrimination in employment is that age discrimination is a victimless crime. Older Americans are often portrayed in the media as living the good life, basking in a sunny clime while sipping a frosty piña colada. This is wishful thinking for most retirees.

As with other age groups, research shows the top ten percent of older Americans hold the vast majority of wealth for their age group.[6] Millions of older workers lost savings, jobs and homes in the Great Recession, just as they were

---

[6] Bruening, Matt. *Wealth is Distributed Extremely Unevenly Within Every Age Group*, Demos (September 8, 2014).

approaching their retirement years. They lacked the time or the ability (due to age discrimination in hiring) to recoup their losses. They have entered or are entering their retirement without sufficient savings to finance two or three years of retirement, let alone several decades.

Meanwhile, traditional pensions virtually disappeared for private sector workers in the 1990s. More than a quarter of private sector workers in 1967 had a traditional defined benefit pension that provided significant income for the duration of their retirement. Today fewer than 14 percent of private sector workers have a defined benefit pension.[7]

> *Age discrimination in employment is a bread and butter issue for many older Americans.*

Social Security benefits represent an increasingly important lifeline for retirees but they are not substantial enough to support a middle-class lifestyle. A third of recipients rely completely on Social Security benefits; two-thirds get at least half of their total income from Social Security. According to the Social Security Administration, the average benefit for a retired person in 2014 was about $1,300 a month or $15,500 a year. This modest benefit dips below the poverty line when medical costs are factored in. The

---

[7] See Employee Benefits Research Institute, *FAQs about benefits: Retirement Issues*, viewed on 12/09/15 at
http://www.ebri.org/publications/benfaq/index.cfm?fa=retfaq14

Kaiser Family Foundation estimated in 2014 that Social Security recipients pay an average annual out of pocket expense of $4,734 for Medicare and Medi-gap health insurance.[8] The official federal poverty level for an individual in 2015 was $11,770.

A growing number of older workers have no choice but to remain in the workplace. They need the money to pay their rent and to buy groceries. Economists estimate the market force participation rate for workers aged 55 and older is projected to grow from 32.4 percent in 2000 to 43 percent in 2020.

Millions of older workers must work long past traditional retirement age to stave off actual poverty.

Age discrimination deprives older workers of their ability to remain in the workforce and stay out of poverty. A 2013 study by the Economic Policy Institute (EPI) found that almost half of all retirees are struggling financially. Twenty million Americans (48 percent) aged 65 and older are considered "economically vulnerable." This is defined as having an income that is less than two times the supplemental poverty threshold (a poverty line more comprehensive than

---

[8] *How Much is Enough? Out-of-Pocket Spending Among Medicare Beneficiaries: A Chartbook*, Kaiser Family Foundation (July 21, 2014), viewed on 12/2/15 at http://kff.org/health-costs/report/how-much-is-enough-out-of-pocket-spending-among-medicare-beneficiaries-a-chartbook/.

the traditional federal poverty line). Elder poverty rates are much higher for women and minorities.

Meanwhile, Americans are living longer in retirement. They must finance more years out of the workforce with less money. When the ADEA was adopted by Congress in 1967, the average life expectancy was 67 years of age for men and 74 years of age for women. Today, the average lifespan for is 76 years for men and 81 years for women.

Age discrimination in employment may actually be more harmful than other types of discrimination because it consigns millions of older workers to poverty and deprivation for the rest of their lives!

Now, the Good News!

At this point, you may be feeling exasperated but rest assured that, despite its many flaws, the ADEA does provide vital protection for older workers.

The ADEA establishes a legal right for workers to be free from age discrimination in employment. It establishes a framework in the federal court system to enforce that right. And while the ADEA permits the imposition of fewer sanctions against discriminatory employers than Title VII, employers still face significant risk.

Despite its flaws, the ADEA offers older workers important protections against age discrimination.

No employer wants to be sued, especially for discrimination. It costs an average of more than $100,000 to defend even a frivolous lawsuit. Moreover, businesses spend millions of dollars annually marketing their brands to foster a positive image. Many experts agree that a business's reputation is its most valuable asset. Once tarnished, a reputation can be extremely difficult- if not impossible- to rebuild. This is why corporations employ large legal departments to handle employment discrimination complaints. Many employers vigorously defend all lawsuits to avoid the prospect of a newspaper headline declaring the company guilty of discrimination.

In addition, the ADEA is not the only game in town. Every state has adopted its own age discrimination law. These laws are patterned after the ADEA but tend to be more generous with respect to the number of employees who are protected and the scope of remedies are available to plaintiffs. Many attorneys prefer to file state age discrimination law claims and to litigate in state courts, where elected judges are thought to be more sympathetic to victims of age discrimination.

More good news may be on the horizon for older workers. The current median age of the U.S. workforce is 42.3, compared to 37.1 in 1992. A 2013 study by the Stanford Center on Longevity projects that workers aged 55 and older will account for 25 percent of the labor force by 2020. Due to changing demographics, employers will need to hire and retain older workers in the future.

Regardless of what the future holds, however, age discrimination in employment will not disappear. There are myriad reasons why employers discriminate on the basis of age. Stores and restaurants, for example, engage in age discrimination to present a "youthful" appearance to the public. Businesses target older workers to cut costs. Experienced workers and workers who have accumulated a significant number of years of service tend to be older workers who are paid more. Unscrupulous employers will continue to exploit every legal loophole.

Meanwhile, society effectively subsidizes discriminatory employers by picking up the cost to provide social services and health care to the victim and his or her family. Society also loses income when these workers are no longer able pay taxes. It's time to end this employer subsidy by insuring equal justice for older workers in the workplace.

If you are facing age discrimination, you can't wait for speculative future changes. The stakes are too high. A job is the sole source of financial security for most Americans and makes it possible for them to obtain health care and to save for retirement. A job is central to an individual's self-esteem, to their role in the family and position in the community.

Moreover, most workers invest the greater part of their lives in their work. At the very least, older workers deserve to be treated fairly. Do not ignore age discrimination. Take it upon yourself to understand, confront and overcome age discrimination.

There is no reason to acquiesce to the inevitability of age discrimination in employment, any more than race or sex discrimination. It is not inevitable! It is a byproduct of unjust social and legal forces that will surely change in time if enough older workers demand change.

DISCLAIMER: This book is meant to be a guide only. The law is fluid. It will change after this book is published as a result of future court rulings, Congressional enactments and/or federal regulation. This book is essentially a snapshot of the law at a particular point in time. This book contains citations to important cases and studies to assist readers who wish to conduct further research. Moreover, be aware that this author's interpretation of legal decisions, events and trends may not be shared by the judge assigned to your case.

2. WHAT IS AGE DISCRIMINATION?

"The jury could have concluded that [the hospital] acted disproportionately by dismissing an employee who had performed well for more than 17 years for returning late from vacation for reasons beyond her control, who could not then immediately return to work because of illness ... and whose lateness in returning did not cause [the hospital] any significant problems."

- *Nembhard v. Mem'l Sloan-Kettering Cancer Ctr.*, 918 F. Supp. 784 (S.D.N.Y. 1996)

Age discrimination occurs when employees, job applicants or union members are treated less favorably because of their age. Not all age discrimination is illegal. For example, it is not illegal for an employer to discriminate against an employee who is under the age of 40.

The U.S. Supreme Court says the ADEA "does not mean to stop an employer from favoring an older employee over a younger one...The enemy of 40 is 30, not 50."[1]

Moreover, not all adverse treatment experienced by older workers is discriminatory. Older workers can be discharged or otherwise disciplined for bad conduct and incompetence, as long as younger workers would receive the same treatment

---

[1] *General Dynamics Land Systems, Inc. v. Cline*, 540 U.S. 581 (2004).

23

under equivalent circumstances. In other words, older workers cannot be singled out for special adverse treatment [2]

> *Whether an action (or inaction) constitutes illegal age discrimination depends upon whether it violates a law.*

Ultimately, age discrimination is illegal when it violates a federal or state law.

The Law

The leading federal law in the United States against age discrimination is the Age Discrimination in Employment Act of 1967 (ADEA).[3]

The ADEA has seemingly specific and clear language for what constitutes illegal age discrimination. However, the U.S. Supreme Court and federal courts in recent years have dramatically narrowed the limited scope of coverage of the ADEA. What Congress set forth in relatively clear language in 1967 is now anything but clear.

The ADEA's substantive provisions break down illegal activity into the following categories: age discrimination by employers, by employment agencies, by labor organizations, and retaliation by all three.

---

[2] 29 U.S.C. Code § 623 (f) (3).
[3] Pub. L. No. 90-202, codified at 29 U.S.C. § 621 through 29 U.S.C. § 634.

➢ General Provisions

Section 623(a-e) of the ADEA states that it is unlawful for employers, employment agencies, and labor organizations to:

- Fail or refuse to hire or to discharge any individual because s/he is aged 40 or above;

- Discriminate against any individual aged 40+ because of the individual's age with respect to compensation, terms, conditions, or privileges of employment;

- Limit, segregate or classify an employee aged 40+ so as to deprive or tend to deprive that individual of employment opportunities or otherwise affect his/her status as an employee. This occurs when an employer unreasonably treats an older worker differently from others with the same job title or in the same work unit who are *not* members of the protected group;

- Retaliate against an individual who oppose age discrimination by complaining or assisting in the investigation or prosecution of an age discrimination claim.

- Print, publish or cause to be published any notice or advertisement that indicates any preference, limitation, specification, or discrimination based on age.

Federal courts have ruled the ADEA, a hybrid of the Fair Labor Standards Act (FLSA), does not permit claims against persons in their individual capacities or class action lawsuits. ADEA plaintiffs can, however, file "collective action" lawsuits in accordance with the FLSA.[4] There are significant differences between class actions and collective actions. It is generally easier to certify a collective action, which requires only that plaintiffs be "similarly situated" and file a written consent with the court to become a plaintiff. The standard for a class action is stricter and requires the named plaintiffs to demonstrate they adequately represent the entire class.

➢ Employment Agencies

Section 623(b) states it is unlawful for employment agencies to:

- Fail or refuse to refer an individual for employment, or otherwise discriminate against any individual, on the basis of age; and

- To cause an employer to engage in age discrimination.

An employment agency is subject to the ADEA if the agency "regularly undertakes with or without compensation"

---

[4] 29 U.S.C. § 216(b).

the procurement of employees for an employer, other than an agency of the United States.

➤ Labor Organizations

Sections 623(c) of the ADEA states the following activities are unlawful if done by labor organizations because of an individual's age:

- To exclude or expel from its membership, limit, segregate, or classify its membership, or

- To classify or fail or refuse to refer for employment any individual, in any way which would deprive or tend to deprive any individual of employment opportunities.

- To adversely affect an individual's status as an employee or an applicant for employment.

- To cause or attempt to cause an employer to discriminate against any individual on the basis of age.

A labor organization is covered by the ADEA if it has at least 25 members and is "engaged in an industry affecting commerce ... and includes any organization of any kind, any agency, or employee representation committee, group, association, or plan . . . dealing with employers concerning grievances, labor disputes, wages, rates of pay, hours, or other terms or conditions of employment."

➤ Retaliation

Finally, Sec. (4) (d) of the ADEA makes it unlawful for an employer, employment agency, or labor organization to:

> Discriminate against employees or applicants for employment [or membership] because the individual... has made a charge, testified, assisted, or participated in any manner in an investigation, proceeding, or litigation under this chapter."

To prove retaliation, plaintiffs must show they suffered an adverse action for engaging in a statutorily protected activity, such as termination or a demotion marked by a decrease in wages or a less distinguished title. Plaintiffs must show the retaliation was the determinative reason for the adverse action and not merely a contributing factor.[5] This "but for" standard of causation requires the plaintiff to show that "but for" the employer's retaliatory motive the adverse action would not have occurred. Receiving a challenging work assignment generally is not considered to be sufficiently adverse to constitute retaliation.[6]

Approximately 40 percent of all employment discrimination claims include a charge of retaliation.

Read more about retaliation in Chapter 18.

---

[5] *Crady v. Liberty Nat'l Bank & Trust Co. of Ind.*, 993 F.2d 132, 136 (7th Cir. 1993).

[6] *See Lapka v. Chertoff*, 517 F.3d 974, 985- 86 (7th Cir. 2008).

Signs of Illegal Termination

Most age discrimination complaints are filed by workers who are terminated.[7] Here are some indicators of a discriminatory termination:

- The employee was fired because he or she violated a rule or policy. However, the employer failed to give the employee any prior notice of the existence of the rule. The rule was not published and distributed to all employees (i.e., through an employee handbook).

- Other employees who violated the rule were treated differently or less severely than the complainant.

- The fired employee did not receive any prior warning for violating the rule. Or the warning occurred more than a year ago.

- If performance is at issue, what kind of performance reviews did the employee receive in the past? It would be a red flag if

---

[7] Schrader, Sara von & Zafar E. Nazarov, Trends and Patterns in Age Discrimination in Employment Act (ADEA Charges, Research on Aging 1-22 (2015).

an employee with a history of stellar evaluations was abruptly fired for a performance-related issue. Was counseling or assistance offered to avoid termination?

Courts look skeptically at employers that adopt progressive disciplinary policies but then disregard these policies, such as when a worker is fired without first being provided a written warning in accordance with company policy.

◆

Incompetence

It is worth emphasizing that the ADEA does not protect older workers who cannot perform their jobs.[8] Baseball teams, for example, are not legally required to retain athletes who can't run to first base or spot a fly ball. Employers can terminate workers of any age who are not competent to perform their job.

At the same time, an employer's expectations should be no greater for older workers than they are for younger workers who are similarly situated. And an older worker should not be subjected to a higher degree of disciplinary action than a similarly situated younger worker. It violates the ADEA to single out an older worker for adverse treatment.

---

[8] 29 U.S.C. Code § 623 (f)(3).

Employers cannot have higher expectations for older workers than they have for younger workers in the same position.

In 2013, a federal appeals court in Philadelphia, PA upheld the termination of a 73-year-old physician by a medical practice for apparent age-related conditions. The court said the physician's firing did not violate either the ADEA or the Americans with Disabilities Act.[9] Dr. Roger Ball sued the medical practice where he worked until 2009 when his contract was not renewed after audits uncovered administrative and patient care problems. He was cited for low productivity, mobility problems relating to a nervous system disorder, failure to proper billing codes and to provide clinical documentation, and over-prescription of narcotics to patients.

He was not treated any differently than younger doctors after deficiencies were discovered.

Ball argued that he was fired due to his advanced age and a physically debilitating affliction, Chronic Inflammatory Demyelinating Polyneuropathy. He said the criticism of his performance was a pretext for age and disability discrimination. The appellate court disagreed.

---

9 *Ball v. Einstein Community Health Associates, Inc.*, NO. 10-cv-2474 (3rd Cir. 2/14/13).

The court found that younger physicians were subjected to the same audit and review procedures as Dr. Ball, and that similar action was taken against them when discrepancies were discovered. The court said the medical practice's business reasons for firing Dr. Ball were legitimate and not a pretext for age discrimination.

Two Types of Age Discrimination

There are two basic types of age discrimination and each has a different method of proof in the federal court system.

1. Disparate *Treatment* Discrimination

More than 98 percent of all discrimination cases involve disparate treatment discrimination or intentional discrimination.[10] An example of disparate treatment discrimination is when an employer fires an older worker because s/he wants to "get rid of deadwood" and hire "new blood."

> "...the essence of age discrimination is 'for an older employee to be fired because the employer believes that productivity and competence decline with old age.'" - U.S. Supreme Court.[11]

---

[10] Nielsen, L.B., et. al, *Contesting Workplace Discrimination in Court; Characteristics and Outcomes of Federal Employment Litigation (1987-2003)*, 11, The American Bar Foundation (October 29, 2008).
[11] *Hazen Paper Co. v. Biggins*, 507 U.S. 604 (1993).

The highest percentage of age discrimination complaints filed with the EEOC each year (63 percent) involve workers who lost their jobs, either through discharge or layoff. But the most pervasive form of age discrimination in the United States probably involves hiring discrimination. Surveys and studies show that age discrimination in hiring is blatant, virtually unchallenged and seemingly epidemic. It is often difficult to prove hiring discrimination because applicants lack access to information about why they didn't get a job.

- For in depth analyses of disparate treatment or intentional discrimination see Chapter 10.

2. Disparate *Impact* discrimination.

This type of discrimination involves a neutral policy that has a disproportionately negative impact on older workers. There is no requirement to prove the employer intended to discriminate. Disparate impact discrimination often involves broad structural disadvantages that are built into employment practices. An example of disparate impact discrimination is when an employer requires applicants for a desk job to run a seven-minute mile. Workers aged 50 or 60 technically are not barred from applying for these positions but they might as well be. Moreover, the running requirement does not bear a reasonable relationship to the duties of the position.

Federal courts have made it very difficult for workers to challenge structural age discrimination in employment so lawsuits alleging disparate impact age discrimination are rare. There is a conflict within federal circuits as to whether older job applicants cannot even file disparate impact lawsuits. Most circuits say no. However, the U.S. Court of Appeals for the 11th Circuit in Atlanta ruled in 2015 that job applicants can file disparate impact lawsuits. This created a split in the federal circuits that only the U.S. Supreme Court can resolve. The 11th Circuit has jurisdiction over Alabama, Florida and Georgia.[12]

-For in depth analysis of disparate impact discrimination, which involves discriminatory policies and practices, see Chapter 15.

Disparate Treatment	Disparate impact
• Employee suffered adverse employment action (i.e., demoted, fired). • Must show the employer intended to discriminate.	• Employer's neutral policy or rule had a different effect on older workers. • No requirement to prove employer intended to discriminate.

✓ Checklist for Age Discrimination

The EEOC says the following actions by employers indicate a pattern of age discrimination:

☐ Younger employees are treated more favorably than older employees under the same circumstances;

---

[12] See *Villarreal v. R.J. Reynolds Tobacco Company, Pinstripe, Inc. CareerBuilder, LLC.*, No. 15-10602 (11th Cir. November 30, 2015)

☐ Older employees suffer stricter consequences for the same behavior engaged in by younger employees;

☐ Older workers who are more qualified than younger employees are passed over for promotions for which they apply;

☐ A supervisor assigns younger workers the best leads and/or equipment;

☐ Older workers are excluded from key meetings;

☐ Owner/manager/supervisor socializes only with the younger employees;

☐ When an older worker hits an age milestone, the employer suddenly changes its attitude, perhaps becoming harsher in employment evaluations and issuing write-ups for behavior that was ignored in the past;

☐ The employer recruits and hires only younger employees.

Federal courts are not required to adhere to the EEOC's checklist but most lend it credence in their evaluations.

Vexing Double Standard

What people think they know about age discrimination is often based on what they know about Title VII of the Civil Rights Act of 1964, which prohibits discrimination on the basis of race, sex, religion, color and national origin. The

ADEA is and always has been far weaker than Title VII. The ADEA both prohibits and legalizes age discrimination. For example, the ADEA legalizes mandatory retirement at age 55 for police, firefighters, border patrol guards, bus drivers and other public safety workers. No medical support establishes age 55 as the point at which public safety workers become unable to adequately perform their job duties.

> *Age discrimination is treated far less severely than discrimination on the basis of race, sex, religion, color and national origin.*

The ADEA has many loopholes and legalizes a broad swath of age discrimination that is illegal under Title VII. Two key differences between the ADEA and Title VII are:

- The ADEA permits employers to engage in age discrimination when it is based on a "reasonable factor other than age."[13] There is no such thing as "reasonable" discrimination under Title VII. If an employer uses a test that has an adverse impact welfareon blacks or women, Title VII requires the employer to show the test is job-related, consistent with "business necessity," and that no less discriminatory alternative was available. Under the ADEA, an employer need only show that age

---

[13] *Smith v. City of Jackson*, 544 U.S. 228 (2005).

discrimination was "reasonably" necessary to the "normal operation" of the particular business. Employers are not required to use the least discriminatory alternative.

- Unlike Title VII, the ADEA does not permit plaintiffs to recover compensatory or punitive damages. The ADEA limits recovery to monetary loss (doubled if the discrimination is found to be willful). If there is no monetary loss, no damages will be awarded.[14] The ADEA minimizes both the pain of age discrimination and the deterrent effect of the law when compared to Title VII.

Age was initially proposed for inclusion as a protected class under Title VII but Congress decided that more study was needed about age discrimination. When Congress finally got around to passing the ADEA three years later, the law was riddled with exceptions, loopholes, and was structurally weaker than Title VII. The ADEA reflects the ageist stereotypes of the 1960s and the influence of big business in Congress. In the 1960s, most women were "housewives" and their husbands retired with a defined benefit pension that

---

[14] See *Andrews v. CBOCS West*, No. 12-3399 (7th Cir.), February 14, 2014. The plaintiff was subjected to daily, derogatory age-based remarks made by her supervisor. However, the U.S. Court of Appeals for the Seventh Circuit found that the plaintiff had voluntarily resigned from employment and, therefore, suffered no materially adverse employment action.

supported both of them in their old age. Times have changed but not the basic tenets of the ADEA.

3. THE AGE DISCRIMINATION IN EMPLOYMENT ACT

The Age Discrimination in Employment Act of 1967 (ADEA) is the main federal law that prohibits age discrimination in employment. It applies to employers throughout the nation who meet threshold eligibility requirements.

Each state has adopted its own age discrimination law and these laws tend to be more generous than the ADEA in terms of who is protected, how age discrimination is defined, the plaintiff's burden of proof, and the amount of damages available to victims. Plaintiff attorneys often prefer state courts but an employer can file a motion to remove a case that is filed in a state court to federal court.

The ADEA prohibits age discrimination in:

- Hiring;
- Firing;
- Compensation;
- Benefit terms; or,
- Any other aspect of employment.

The ADEA protects individuals who are aged 40 and above and who are employees, job applicants, members of or applicants for membership to labor organization, and individuals seeking a referral from employment agencies. It also protects individuals who complain about age discrimination or assist in the investigation or prosecution of an age discrimination claim.

> *The ADEA provides the minimum amount of protection against age discrimination in employment. State age discrimination laws tend to be more generous.*

Initially, the ADEA covered employees between the ages of 40 and 65. The upper limit was extended to 70 in 1978 and then, in 1986, was removed completely. But the lower age limit has remained the same. Workers generally are not protected by the ADEA unless they were aged 40 or above when the age discrimination occurred. There are exceptions, including:

- The ADEA covers discriminatory acts that occurred prior to a worker's 40th birthday if it is part of a continuing violation where at least one discriminatory act occurred within the statute of limitations.[1]

- The age requirement is waived for individuals under the age of 40 who are subject to retaliation for opposing a practice made unlawful by the ADEA, including individuals who testified, assisted or participated in an investigation or an age discrimination lawsuit. [2]

➢ Covered EMPLOYERS

As previously noted, employers are not subject to the ADEA unless they are "engaged in an industry affecting commerce" and have 20 or more employees "for each working day in each of twenty or more calendar weeks in the current or preceding calendar year."[3] However, some employers who meet these criteria are nevertheless exempt from the ADEA. For example, the U.S. Supreme Court ruled in 2000 that the doctrine of sovereign immunity provides that states cannot be ordered to pay monetary damages to state employees in a federal ADEA lawsuit.[4] States are essentially

---

[1]See *National Railroad Passenger Corp. (Amtrak) v. Morgan*, 536 U.S. 101 (2002).

[2] 29 U.S.C. Code § 623 (d).

[3] 29 U.S.C. Code § 623 (a-c).

[4] *Kimel v. Florida Bd. of Regents*, 528 U.S. 62 (2000). Holding that Congress exceeded its power to enforce the Fourteenth Amendment by prohibiting age discrimination by the states.

exempt from the ADEA unless the state has waived its right to sovereign immunity under the Eleventh Amendment of the U.S. Constitution.

Cities and local governments can be sued for damages under the ADEA because they are deemed to be sufficiently independent of the state to be eligible for coverage under the state's sovereign immunity.[5]

Federal employees are protected from age discrimination under a separate "federal sector" provision of the ADEA. There are significant differences between the federal sector provisions of the ADEA and the ADEA as it applies to other workers.[6] For example, the federal sector ADEA, 29 U.S.C. §633 (a), states that all federal personnel actions "shall be made free from any discrimination based on age." A federal agency can be found liable for any amount of age discrimination in an adverse employment action, whereas the ADEA requires private sector workers to prove that age discrimination was the determinative cause of the adverse employment decision. As a result, private sector workers can lose an ADEA case even after showing the existence of age discrimination.

---

[5] See *Evans v. City of Bishop*, 238 F. 3rd 586, 586-590 (5th Cir. 2001).
[6] 29 U.S.C. § 633(a).

Employees of the U.S. House of Representatives and U.S. Senate are protected from age discrimination under the Congressional Accountability Act of 1995.[7]

Individual supervisors and managers can be sued in some federal circuits under Title VII but they are not considered "employers" who are subject to liability under the ADEA.

> ## To be subject to the ADEA an employer must be:
>
> - Engaged in an industry affecting commerce;
>
> - Have 20 or more employees for each working day for at least 20 calendar weeks in the current or preceding year; and,
>
> - Have an employment relationship with the claimed employee.

'Twenty-Plus' Rule

At first glance, it may seem that an employer is exempt from the ADEA because the business does not employ 20 or more workers as required under the ADEA. When counting the number of employees, however, plaintiffs may include

---

[7] 2 U.S.C.A. §1301.

43

employees who work for entities that are related to the employer, such as parent and subsidiary companies and sister corporations.

Courts have even ruled that shareholders, owners and directors may be considered "employees" rather than employers in some circumstances.[8]

See Chapter 6 for a discussion of the Joint Employer Liability Doctrine, which permits multiple employers that each have fewer than 20 employees to be considered the legal equivalent of a single or joint employer for the purpose of meeting the ADEA's 20+ employee rule.

The 20+ rule represents a higher bar than a similar rule contained in Title VII's of the Civil Rights Act of 1964, which prohibits discrimination on the basis of race, sex, religion, color and national origin. Title VII requires an employer to employ only 15 or more workers.

The Pizza Parlor across Town

A restaurant with 15 employees changes its "theme" and requires all servers to wear a uniform that consists of tight fitting T-shirts and short-shorts.

---

[8] See *Raymond B. Yates, M.D., P.C., Profit Sharing Plan v. Hendon*, 541 U.S. 1 (2004).

A 56-year-old female server who has worked at the restaurant for decades is fired because she does not look good in the new "uniform."

Since the restaurant has fewer than 20 employees, it appears to fall outside the parameters of the ADEA. However, the owner also owns a pizza parlor across town that employs seven workers. The number of workers at both restaurants, when added together, satisfies the threshold number of employees required to bring the employer within the purview of the ADEA.

The employer can be sued under the ADEA for age discrimination.

➤ Covered EMPLOYEES

The ADEA defines an "employee" as an individual who works for or has worked for an employer or has applied for employment. The ADEA was extended to cover union apprenticeship programs in 1996.

A common defense to ADEA lawsuits is that the plaintiff is not eligible to evoke the protection of the ADEA because s/he is or was not in an "employment relationship" with the employer.

➤ Test for an Employment Relationship

To be subject to the ADEA, an employment relationship must exist between an employer and an employee at the time of the alleged discrimination.

The fact that a worker has signed an agreement stating that s/he is an independent contractor may not settle the matter. The reality of the working relationship– not the label attached to it– is what counts. The existence of an employment relationship depends on the degree to which the employer controls the means and manner of an employee's work performance.

According to the EEOC, some or all of the following factors may be relevant in determining when a worker is in an employment relationship with an employer:

- The employer has the right to exercise control over when, where, and how the worker performs the job.

- The employer furnishes the tools, materials, and equipment.

- The work is performed on the employer's premises.

- There is a continuing relationship between the worker and the employer.

- The employer has the right to assign additional projects to the worker.

- The employer sets the hours of work and the duration of the job.

- The worker is paid by the hour, week or month rather than the agreed cost of performing a particular job.

- The worker does not hire and pay assistants.

- The work performed by the worker is part of the regular business of the employer.

- The worker is not engaged in his/her own distinct occupation or business.

- The employer provides the worker with benefits such as insurance, leave, or workers' compensation.

- The worker is considered an employee of the employer for tax purposes (i.e., the employer withholds federal, state, and Social Security taxes).

- The employer can discharge the worker.

- The worker and the employer believe that they have created an employer-employee relationship.

The above list is not exhaustive and the EEOC states that showing some or even a majority of the listed criteria does not automatically prove or disprove the existence of an employment relationship.[9]

Contractor v. Employee

Mary, 52, a computer software engineer, was hired as an independent contractor by a major computer software company. She worked full-time under the supervision of a company manager who made her assignments and evaluated her performance. She was assigned a desk and was expected to work there weekdays from 9 a.m. to 5 p.m. Her co-workers were full-time employees who did equivalent work but received health and retirement benefits and were paid twice as much. Mary was told that her services were no longer required but she found out that she had been replaced by a much younger, less experienced worker. Mary can argue that she was a company employee who was misclassified as an independent contractor. As a company employee, she would be entitled to sue for age discrimination under the ADEA.

♦

---

[9] *See* EEOC Compliance Manual, Title VII, Section 2, Threshold Issues, downloaded on 7/3/15 from
http://www.eeoc.gov/policy/docs/threshold.html.

Outside the Umbrella of the ADEA

Here is a list of workers who are partially or wholly exempt from the protection of the ADEA:

- ✓ Owners of enterprises.
- ✓ Directors.
- ✓ Partners.
- ✓ State and local elected officials, their personal staffs, and high-policy making employees.[10]
- ✓ Older worker who are discharged or otherwise disciplined for good cause.[11]
- ✓ Governmental bodies can limit the age of hire of federal, state, and local law enforcement officers and firefighters and can force them to retire at age 55 pursuant to a bona fide hiring or retirement plan that is not a subterfuge to evade the purposes of the ADEA.[12]
- ✓ Bona fide executives or employees working in high policy-making positions are subject to mandatory retirements for the two-year period immediately before retirement if they have attained the age of 65 and are entitled to retirement benefits of at least

---

[10]29 U.S. Code § 630 (f).
[11] 29 U.S.C. Code § 623 (f)(3).
[12] 29 U.S.C. Code § 623 (j).

$44,000 (excluding Social Security benefits and former and current employer contributions).[13]

✓ Independent contractors are not "employees" (though courts will review whether a worker has been misclassified as an independent contractor).[14]

✓ An employer, employment agency or labor organization in a foreign country can discriminate on the basis of age where to do otherwise would violate the law of the country in which the workplace is located.[15]

✓ State employees cannot sue a state under the ADEA unless the state has waived its right to sovereign immunity. In other words, a state employee cannot sue a state for monetary damages in a federal court without the state's consent.[16] The EEOC can file a discrimination lawsuit against any state whether or not the state has waived its sovereign immunity.

✓ Treaties can limit the scope of protection under the ADEA for employees who work in the United States for foreign employers.

---

[13] 29 U.S. Code § 631 (c)(1).

[14] See *E.E.O.C. v. North Knox School Corp.*, 154 F.3d 744, 746-47 (7th Cir. 1998).

[15] 29 U.S.C. §623(f) (1).

[16] See *Kimel v. Florida Board of Regent*, 528 U.S. 62 (2000)).

- ✓ The EEOC can create administrative exceptions to the ADEA for programs of public employment serving "the long-term unemployed, handicapped, members of minority groups, older workers, or youth."[17]

- ✓ The Higher Education Amendments of 1998 allow institutions of higher education to offer tenured professors "supplemental benefits" to encourage them to accept voluntary age-based early retirement incentive plans. These added benefits must be in addition to normal retirement or severance benefits. The amendments replaced language in the ADEA that permitted mandatory retirement of tenured professors at age 65.

- ✓ Distinctions based on age can be made where age is a "bona fide occupational qualification" that is "reasonably related" to the normal operation of a particular business.[18]

- ✓ Age discrimination can be based on a "reasonable factor other than age."[19]

- ✓ Certain age-based distinctions can be made pursuant to a bona fide seniority system and with respect to a

---

[17] 29 U.S.C. § 628 (2006).
[18] 29 U.S.C. § 623(f)(1).
[19] 29 U.S.C. § 623(f)(1).

voluntary early retirement incentive plan or an employment benefit plan.[20]

✓ Some courts have refused to enforce the ADEA with respect to actions by ministers or religious organizations that relate to the exercise of religious doctrine or practice.

✓ The EEOC contends the ADEA "presumptively" applies to Native American tribes unless its application would infringe upon treaty rights or tribal sovereignty.[21]

Some of the above exceptions are subject to challenge. For example, the EEOC has filed age discrimination lawsuits in recent years against law firms that labelled employees as "partners" to avoid being subject to the ADEA. Similarly, courts have ruled in favor of independent contractors who argued they were employees who were improperly categorized by employers to save money.

No Way to Treat a Partner!

Fred was hired as "partner" at a law firm. However, Fred had no decision-making authority, no

---

[20] 29 U.S.C. § 623(f), (i), (l).
[21] *See* EEOC Compliance Manual, downloaded on 7/4/15 from http://www.eeoc.gov/policy/docs/threshold.html#2-III-B-2-b.

job security and he was paid a salary rather than a percentage of the profits.

Years later, when Fred turned age 65, members of the executive council pressured him to retire. Fred refused and was subsequently fired for "performance issues."

Fred filed an age discrimination lawsuit, which the firm sought to dismiss the lawsuit on the grounds that Fred, as a partner, was exempt from the protection of the ADEA.

Courts have ruled that employees like Fred were actually employees, not partners, and therefore were entitled to the protection of the ADEA.

♦

Are you protected?

➢ Were you age 40 or older when the discrimination occurred?

➢ Were you in an employment relationship with the employer at the time?

➢ Are you or your employer exempt from the protection of the ADEA? (i.e. independent contractor, state employee, high ranking executive.)

---

4. WAIVER OF ADEA RIGHTS

The ADEA contemplates that employees may wish to waive their rights to the protection of the ADEA.[44] Why would older workers want to waive their rights under the ADEA? There are many reasons, including:

- Employers often ask older workers to waive their ADEA rights to participate in a "golden parachute" exit termination or retirement plan.

- Plaintiffs in age discrimination cases may waive their rights under the ADEA to settle an age discrimination complaint.

The EEOC is not bound by a waiver signed by an employee and can litigate a claim of age discrimination even if the plaintiff decides not to do so.

Is the Waiver Voluntary?

Sometimes workers waive their ADEA rights without realizing what they are giving up, because they feel pressured to do so. Other times a worker may learn after executing a waiver that s/he was a victim of age discrimination.

When a waiver is disputed, courts will consider all relevant factors— the totality of the circumstances-- to

---

[44] 29 U. S.C. 626(f).

determine whether the employee knowingly and voluntarily waived the right to sue under the ADEA. If the court finds the worker signed the waiver without understanding the terms or that the waiver was involuntary, it can be declared invalid.

The U.S. Congress amended the ADEA in 1990 by passing the Older Workers Benefits Protection Act (OWBPA) to halt abusive practices with respect to waivers. The OWBPA states that an individual "may not waive any right or claim under [the ADEA] unless the waiver is knowing and voluntary."[45] The OWBPA is intended to insure that older workers have complete and accurate information about their benefits and are not pressured into waiving their rights.

➢ Requirements for Voluntariness

The OWBPA sets forth minimal requirements that an employer must take to insure a waiver is knowing and voluntary: A waiver must be

A. Written in a manner calculated to be understood by the individual or by the average individual who is eligible to participate in the waiver;

B. Specifically refer to rights or claims arising under the ADEA;

---

[45] 29 U.S.C. §626(f) (1).

C. Cannot waive rights or claims that may arise after the date the waiver is executed;

D. Be in exchange for consideration above and beyond anything the individual already is entitled to;

E. Advise the individual to consult with an attorney before signing the waiver;

F. Provide at least 21 days to consider the agreement; or 45 days if the waiver is requested in connection with an employment termination program that is offered to a group or class of employees;

G. Can be revoked by the signer at any time during the seven-day period after signing;

H. For a waiver that is sought in connection with a group plan, the employer must state the eligibility factors and time limits for the plan and provide the job titles and ages of individuals who are both eligible and not eligible to participate in the plan.

If validity of a waiver is disputed, the employer – "the party asserting the validity of a waiver" – has the burden of proving the waiver was made knowingly and voluntarily.[46]

---

[46] 29 U. S.C. 626(f)(3).

No Shortcuts on Waivers

Dolores Oubre, a scheduler at a power plant run by Entergy Operations, Inc. in Killona, LA, received a poor performance rating. Her supervisor gave her the option of improving her performance or accepting a voluntary severance agreement. She was given a packet of information about the severance agreement and told that she had 14 days to decide whether to sign. After consulting with an attorney, Oubre accepted the severance package.

Oubre signed the agreement, including a release in which she "agree[d] to waive, settle, release, and discharge any and all claims, demands, damages, actions, or causes of action . . . that I may have against Entergy . . ." In exchange, she received six installment payments over the next four months totaling $6,258.

Oubre subsequently filed a lawsuit against Entergy for age discrimination in violation of the ADEA.

In 1998, the U.S. Supreme Court ruled in *Oubre v. Entergy Operations, Inc.* that Entergy had not complied with three of the requirements of the OWBPA waiver provisions:[47] Oubre was not given enough time to consider her options; provided seven days after signing the release to change her mind; and the release lacked a specific reference to the ADEA.

"Congress imposed specific duties on employers who seek releases of certain claims created by statute. Congress delineated these duties with precision and without qualification: An employee 'may not waive' an ADEA claim unless the employer complies with the statute. Courts cannot with ease presume ratification of that which Congress forbids," said the Court.

The Court permitted Oubre to keep the money she received as part of a severance agreement.

♦

The EEOC recognizes that older workers often need severance payments to pay for living expenses. Therefore, EEOC regulations state the contract principles of "tender back" (returning the consideration received for the waiver before challenging it in court) and "ratification" (approving or ratifying the waiver by retaining the consideration) do not apply with respect to waivers of the ADEA. In other words,

---

[47] 522 U.S. 422 (1998).

if a waiver is found to be invalid, the payee is not required to return any funds received pursuant to the waiver.

What is 'Knowing'?

A waiver must be both knowing and voluntary. The term 'knowing' signifies that the waiver was written in such a way that the signer can understand its terms and the consequences of signing the waiver. This is not simply a matter of using clear language.

An appellate court held that a waiver was not knowing and voluntary even though it was unambiguous in *Torrez v. Public Service Company of New Mexico, Inc.*[48]

David Torrez, a foreman for Public Service Company of New Mexico, was told the company was downsizing. He was given 30 days to decide whether he wanted to be voluntarily or involuntarily separated from the company. Torrez chose voluntary separation in exchange for severance pay and additional retirement benefits. He signed a waiver stating: "I . . . hereby release and discharge [my employer] from any and all claims which I have or might have, arising out of or related to my employment or resignation or termination."

Torrez subsequently filed a discrimination lawsuit alleging that he was terminated because of his race and national origin. The appeals court said Torrez' waiver was *not*

---

[48] 908 F.2d 687 (10th Cir. 1990).

knowing and voluntary even though it contained language that was "clear and unambiguous."

An employee must be capable of understanding the waiver agreement.

The waiver failed to specifically mention the release of employment discrimination claims and Torrez testified that he believed that he only was giving up his right to file a lawsuit arising from his voluntary termination and the benefits package he accepted. "This is not an unreasonable conclusion for a high school educated employee, unfamiliar with the law," said the court.

The court also noted that Torrez did not consult with an attorney prior to signing the release, nor was he advised to do so, and that Torrez felt economic duress to accept the voluntary separation because he was not eligible for retirement.

"Under the totality of the circumstances, the evidence ... presented a material question of fact as to whether Torrez knowingly and voluntarily signed the release," writes the court.

5. PARTNERSHIPS

Some employers bestow the title of "partner" on a worker specifically to make them exempt from the protection of the ADEA. Less frequently, a partner claims the status of an employee to secure the benefits of the ADEA. Unfortunately, employers in the legal, accounting and medical professions seem to be particularly prone to these schemes.

Partner in Name Only

One egregious example of the fake partner scam involves a prestigious Chicago-based international law firm, Sidley Austin Brown & Wood. The Equal Employment Opportunity Commission accused Sidley of age discrimination in 2007 after the firm selected 32 partners for termination because of their age.

If a 'partner' has no voice over control of the firm, s/he is probably an employee.

The EEOC's investigation showed that "whatever titles Sidley had decided to give these lawyers - partner, counsel, or otherwise - our investigation indicated that they had no voice or control in governance of the firm and that they could be and were fired just like any other employees without notice and without the vote or consent of their fellow attorneys. A small self-perpetuating group of managers at the top ran everything, and that was the end of the story."

Sidley agreed to a settle the case by paying out damages of $27.5 million.

➢ Test for Partnership

So who exactly is a "partner" under the ADEA? The U.S. Supreme Court defined the elements of true partnership in *Clackamas Gastroenterology v. Wells,* a 2003 case involving four physicians who were director-shareholders of a medical clinic in Oregon.[1] After he was fired, the clinic's bookkeeper filed an age discrimination lawsuit against the clinic. The doctors claimed the clinic could not be sued because it employed fewer 20 employees. However, the bookkeeper argued the doctors should be counted as employees – not partners – which would bring the number of employees over the minimum threshold for ADEA jurisdiction.

The U.S. Supreme Court issued a decision that set forth criteria to assess when a partner also qualifies as an employee under civil rights law. The Court noted that some partnerships have hundreds of partners who are essentially employees who report to a small number of managing partners.

---

[1] *Clackamas Gastroenterology v. Wells,* 538 U.S. 440 (2003).

> *Whether a partner should be counted as an employee depends on the extent of his or her "control" over the business.*

In a 7-2 ruling, the Court said the following factors are relevant as to whether a partner can be considered an employee:

1. Can the organization hire or fire the individual or set rules and regulations governing the individual's work?

2. To what extent does the organization supervise the individual's work?

3. Does the individual report to someone higher up in the organization?

4. Does the individual influence the direction of the organization?

5. Did the parties intend that the individual be an employee, as expressed in a written agreement or contract?

6. Does the individual share in the profits, losses, and liabilities of the organization?

The Court sent the case back to the trial court for additional consideration in keeping with its decision, finding the record contained conflicting evidence as to whether the physicians could be considered true partners.

➤ Discriminating Against Former Partners

The case of Kelley Drye & Warren was unusual in that it involved former equity partners who were victims of age discrimination. The New York City–based international law firm essentially fired equity partner attorneys when they reached the age of 70. The firm forced equity partners to relinquish all of their equity interest in the firm as well as all authority to influence the law firm's operations. Moreover, those who continued to work for the firm received substantially reduced compensation in the form of a discretionary annual bonus.

The EEOC in 2010 charged that the firm "significantly undercompensated" attorneys "solely on the basis of their age."

After forcing equity partners to retire, the law firm paid them lower wages.

The case arose when Eugene T. D'Abelmont, 79, an attorney and former equity partner who specialized in employment law, filed an EEOC complaint on behalf of himself and others.[2] D'Abelmont regularly obtained over $1 million in fees annually from his clients but his compensation was substantially less than younger lawyers at the firm with similar productivity. Moreover, after D'Abelmont complained

---

[2] *EEOC v. Kelley Drye & Warren*, No. 10-CV-0655 (S.D. N.Y. 2010).

internally about the firm's discriminatory age-based compensation system, the firm reduced his bonus payment by two-thirds even though his productivity remained the same.

The firm agreed to settle the case pursuant to the following (painfully humiliating) terms:

- The firm paid D'Abelmont $574,000 for past legal work and agreed to pay him 12 percent of future fees collected from his work for the firm.

- The firm pledged to stop reducing partner pay based solely on age.

- All current partners were required to participate in a mandatory, two-hour sensitivity training on discrimination.

- Members of the firm's executive committee members also were required to participate in an additional one-hour training "on federal laws prohibiting discrimination in employment, with special emphasis on the ADEA."

Partner or Employee?

Occasionally a partner tries to claim the status of an employee to secure the benefits and protections of civil rights law.

In the case of *Solon v. Kaplan*, the U.S. Court of Appeals for the Seventh Circuit in Chicago found that a partner in a small law firm who claimed to be an employee really was a partner and thus not entitled to sue the firm under Title VII of the Civil Rights Act of 1964.[3]

James Solon charged his fellow partners at the law firm of Adler, Kaplan & Begy with terminating his interest in the firm in retaliation for his opposition to sexual harassment. Solon said he was fired because he complained about one of the other partner's alleged sexual harassment of two of the firm's secretaries.

Partners have decision-maker authority, controlling ownership, receive a percentage of the profits, and have employment security.

The appeals court decided that Solon was a partner in the firm because he could only be fired through a two-thirds vote of the general partners. He also held one-fourth of the power to allocate the firm's profits, make financial commitments, amend the partnership agreement, and dissolve the firm. The court said Solon's extent of control in the firm

---

[3] 398 F.3d 629, 633 (7th Cir. 2005).

demonstrated that Solon was a partner and not an employee.

6. THE JOINT EMPLOYER DOCTRINE

'[C]lever men may easily conceal their motivations . . . .'"
- *United States v. City of Black Jack*, 508 F.2d 1179, 1185
(8th Cir. 1974)

Suppose you work in fast-food restaurant alongside a half-dozen coworkers and you are a victim of age discrimination. Your employer appears to have fewer than the minimum threshold number of 20+ employees required to be subject to the ADEA. But appearances can be deceiving. You may still be able to file an ADEA lawsuit under the Joint Employer Doctrine.

The NLRB says two (or more) separate entities can be the equivalent of one employer.

In the summer of 2015, the National Labor Relations Board (NLRB) adopted a new standard to determine whether two or more companies can be considered joint employers of a single workforce.[52] The NLRB is an independent federal agency that safeguards employees' rights to organize collectively and to improve their working conditions. Previously, the NLRB held that an entity was not a joint employer unless it exerted direct and immediate control over

---

[52] *Browning-Ferris Industries*, 362 N.L.R.B. No. 186 (Aug. 27, 2015).

the working conditions of the other entity's employees. Under the new standard, two separate entities are joint employers of a single workforce if they 'share or codetermine those matters governing the essential terms and conditions of employment.'"

The new standard was announced in a case involving a large employer and a staffing agency.

The NLRB ruled that Browning-Ferris Industries (BFI) was the joint employer of the 240 employees hired by staffing agency Leadpoint Business Services to clean and sort recycled products at BFI. A Teamsters local sought to represent the Leadpoint employees and wanted to force BFI to the bargaining table as a "joint employer" of the workers in question. The NLRB ruled 3-2 that BFI qualified as a joint employer because it exercised authority over and reserved the right to control the essential terms and conditions of employment of the Leadpoint employees.

➤ Joint Employer Test

According to the NLRB, a joint employer relationship is indicated when one company shares or codetermines matters governing the essential terms and conditions of employment for the employees of another company. To assess whether an employer possesses sufficient control over the other company's employees, the NLRB considers whether an employer meaningfully affects or influences another company with respect to:

- ✓ Hiring.
- ✓ Firing.
- ✓ Discipline.
- ✓ Supervising and directing workers.
- ✓ Wages and compensation.
- ✓ The number of vacancies to be filled.
- ✓ Setting work hours.
- ✓ Assignment of work and equipment.
- ✓ Determining tenure of employment.

Franchisors

The applicability of the Joint Employer Doctrine frequently arises involves with respect to franchisor/franchisee relationships, especially in the fast-food industry.

In April 2015, the NLRB issued an advisory memorandum addressing when franchisors can be considered joint employers with their franchisees.

The NLRB said Freshii Development, LLC, was not a joint employer with franchisee, Nutritionality, Inc., a Chicago restaurant charged with unfair labor practices. In 2014, Nutritionality terminated one employee and disciplined and terminated another for attempting to unionize its small workforce of five employees.

The NLRB said Freshii was not a joint employer because it did not exercise sufficient control over its franchisees. Freshii provided its franchise restaurant operators with a sample employee handbook and a manual containing personnel policies but there was no evidence that it required franchisees to follow the policies. The NLRB ruled that Freshii did not directly or indirectly control the terms and conditions of employment of the franchisee employees. Therefore, Freshii could not be held responsible for Nutritionality's alleged unfair labor practice.

Veil of Protection

The new interpretation of the Joint Employer Doctrine represents an effort by the NLRB to pierce the "veil of protection" that some employers build into contractor and franchise relationships to avoid liability for violating labor and civil rights laws.

The NLRB ruled in 2014 that CNN, the cable news giant, was a joint employer of a unionized subcontractor, Team Video Services (TVS). The NLRB found that CNN reorganized its operations in 2003 for the purpose of getting rid of TVS, an affiliate of the Communications Workers of America. The NLRB ordered CNN to rehire 100 employees and to compensate 200 workers who remained at TVS without the benefits of a union contract. The NLRB also ordered CNN to resume bargaining with the union.

Is McDonalds a franchisor of fast food restaurants or a risk adverse joint employer?

A national movement has been underway for several years to improve pay and working conditions at fast food restaurants. The NLRB issued 13 complaints in 2014 that named McDonalds, USA, LLC, as the joint employer of more than 70 McDonalds' franchises across the country. The complaints allege that McDonalds and its franchisees violated the rights of restaurant workers by making statements and taking actions against them for participating in nationwide protests. Since 2012, almost 300 charges of labor violations have been filed with the NLRB by fast food workers.

McDonalds contends that 90 percent of the company's more than 14,000 U.S. restaurants are franchisees who set wages and control working conditions within their restaurants. However, the NLRB said its investigation found that McDonalds "engages in sufficient control over its franchisees' operations, beyond protection of the brand, to make it a putative joint employer with its franchisees, sharing liability for [labor law] violations." The NLRB cited

McDonald's use of tools, resources and technology to control franchisees.

Though McDonalds faces a fine of only $50,000, it has spent millions battling the NLRB's joint employer designation. The battle is expected to continue in the courts.

7. INTERNATIONAL CONSIDERATIONS

Initially, the ADEA was silent about whether it applied to American employers with operations outside the United States. The U.S. Congress amended the ADEA in 1984 to include within the definition of employee "any individual who is a citizen of the United States employed by an employer in a workplace in a foreign country." Today, all U.S. citizens who are employed outside the U.S. by a U.S. employer- or a foreign company controlled by an U.S. employer- are protected by the ADEA.

An employer is a U.S. employer if it is incorporated or based in the United States or if it has sufficient connections to the United States. A company has sufficient connections if its principle place of business in the U.S. or the nationality of its dominant shareholders and management is American.

American employers abroad are not required to comply with the ADEA if adherence to that requirement would violate a law of the country where the workplace is located.

U.S. 'Control' over Foreign Corp

A foreign workplace that is controlled by a U.S.

employer is subject to the ADEA. Whether an American employer "controls" a foreign corporation for the purposes of the ADEA depends on:

1. The employer's interrelation of operations with the foreign entity;

2. The extent that both have common management;

3. Whether there exists centralized control of labor relations; and

4. The existence of common ownership or financial control of the employer and the corporation.[1]

> **The appeals court ruled the ADEA covers the American operations of overseas enterprises.**

➢ Non-U.S.Employers Operating in the U.S.

A federal appeals court ruled in 1998 that the ADEA also applies to American workers who are employed in the U.S. by overseas corporations.[2] The case involved a worker who was fired without explanation at the only American branch of a Luxembourg.

Although the bank's U.S. branch had fewer than 20 employees, the Court said the number of the bank's employees world-wide was the important consideration when

---

[11] 29 U.S.C. § 623 (h) (3).
[2] *Morelli v. Cedel*, 141 F.3d 39 (2d Cir. 1998).

determining whether the bank employed the minimal number of workers to be subject to the ADEA. The corporations' number of workers world-wide far exceeded 20 employees.

➢ Treaties and Foreign Employers

Foreign companies have limited liability under American civil rights law if they are parties to a Friendship, Commerce and Navigation (FCN) Treaty, an international agreement that is intended to encourage foreign investment in the United States. FCN treaties permit foreign companies operating in the United States to employ managerial, professional, and other specialized personnel "of their choice." As a result, foreign companies can bypass American workers and hire or promote top executives from their own countries for leadership positions within their U.S. operations.

> *Some courts say U.S. subsidiaries of foreign corporations can be held liable for intentional discrimination.*

However, some courts take the position that even a foreign corporation cannot *intentionally* discriminate on the basis of age.

Korean Air Lines (KAL) in 1988 dismissed all of its American sales managers in a reorganization of its U.S. operations. Employee Thomas MacNamara, 57, who was replaced by a 42-year-old Korean citizen, complained that KAL violated the ADEA. KAL argued that its conduct was privileged under the terms of its FCN Treaty with the United States.

The appeals court said an FCN treaty allows a foreign entity to favor its own citizens when making personnel decisions but it does not shelter the entity from allegations of intentional age discrimination.[3] At the same time, the court said, MacNamara failed to show that Korean Airlines had intentionally discriminated against him.

As long as a foreign company doesn't intentionally discriminate, the court said, the company is entitled under an FCN Treaty to make a personnel decision based on citizenship even if that decision has a disparate or disproportionate impact on older managers who are not from Korea.

---

[3] *MacNamara v. Korean Air Lines*, 863 F.2d 1135 (3d Cir. 1988).

8. FILING AN EEOC COMPLAINT

"No one saves us but ourselves. No one can and no one may. We ourselves must walk the path." – *The Buddha*

Age discrimination victims must exhaust so-called administrative remedies before a federal court can exercise subject matter jurisdiction over their claim.

Under 29 U.S.C. § 626, private sector workers must file a charge with the Equal Employment Opportunity Commission (EEOC) within 180 days of the alleged discrimination. They must then wait at least 60 days before filing an ADEA lawsuit in federal court. If the worker lives in a state that has a state law prohibiting age discrimination and a stage agency that enforces the law, the 180-day deadline is extended to 300 days or 30 days after receipt of notice of termination of state proceedings, whichever is earlier.

The first stop on the journey of an age victim to federal court is the EEOC.

Federal sector workers and job applicants have two options. Under 29 C.F.R § 1614.105, they can invoke an administrative dispute resolution process. If they choose this route, they must contact an EEO officer at the agency where the alleged discrimination occurred within 45 days of the alleged discriminatory act. Alternatively, under 29 U.S.C. § 633 (a)(d), federal workers can file a federal lawsuit. They must file a notice with the EEOC stating their intent to file a lawsuit within 180 after the alleged discriminatory act. Then they must wait at least 30 days until they can file the lawsuit.

The EEOC was created pursuant to Title VII of the Civil Rights Act of 1964 to eliminate unlawful employment discrimination. It is led by a five-member, bipartisan panel and has 53 field offices around the country and about 2,000 employees. The ADEA originally was under the purview of the U.S. Department of Labor (DOL) but responsibility for the ADEA was transferred to the EEOC in 1978 as part of a government consolidation plan.

To file a charge with the EEOC, complainants must complete a Charge Intake Questionnaire that, among other things, asks for a statement of facts of the case. Complainants must identify the parties and describe the alleged discriminatory action. The EEOC uses the form to prepare a formal Charge of Discrimination that it sends to the employee to review, make any corrections, date and sign. The charge is also sent to the employer, which typically files a position statement responding to the allegations.

It is critical for complainants to carefully draft their complaint. Failure to do so could result in the effective dismissal of the charge by the EEOC at the intake state. Also, courts can choose to disregard later allegations unless they could have been discovered in an EEOC investigation of the initial charges. So if a complaint alleges only age discrimination in the EEOC complaint, the plaintiff may be unable to later raise a claim of retaliation.

➤ Statute of Limitations

The importance of adhering to the EEOC's filing deadlines cannot be overstated. Failure to do so could result in the immediate dismissal of a valid age discrimination claim. Unfortunately, the rule governing the statute of limitations for filing a charge with the EEOC is complicated. It is easy to err. If you have any doubt about the statute of limitations in your case, contact the EEOC for clarification.

Again here are the deadlines for filing a private sector ADEA complaint with the EEOC:

- ♦ A charge must be filed with the EEOC within 180 days from the date of the alleged ADEA violation;[1] or

- ♦ Within 300 days after the last discriminatory act if the complaint is filed in a state that has a state age discrimination law and a state agency that enforces the law; or

---

[1] . 29 U.S.C. § 626 (d).

◆ Within 30 days after the complainant receives a notice of termination of proceedings by a state Fair Employment Practices Agency (FEPA).

◆ Federal employees and federal job applicants must contact an agency equal employment opportunity counselor within 45 days.

To avoid duplication of resources, the EEOC maintains "work sharing" collaborations with FEPAs. An age discrimination charge that is filed with either the EEOC or a state FEPA is considered to have been automatically filed with the other agency.[2] FEPAs contract with the EEOC to investigate and charges on behalf of the EEOC.

➢ Filing an EEOC Charge

Employers occasionally try to dismiss age discrimination lawsuits by arguing the plaintiff failed to lodge a valid charge with the EEOC.

The U.S. Supreme Court ruled in 2008 that a filing with the EEOC constitutes a valid charge if it is:

1. In writing;
2. Includes an allegation of discrimination;
3. Names the charged respondent; and
4. Can be "reasonably construed as a request for the [EEOC] to take remedial action to protect the

---

[2] 29 U.S.C. § 633 (b).

employee's rights or otherwise settle a dispute between the employer and the employee."[3]

In Federal *Express Corp. v. Holowecki*, the Court ruled 7-2 that a former employee had filed a valid EEOC charge when he filed an intake questionnaire supported by a detailed affidavit. The Court said a document filed with the EEOC that asks the Agency to protect a worker's rights or to settle a dispute with the employer is a valid discrimination charge under the ADEA.

It is advisable to include the full name, address, and telephone number of the charging party, full name and address of the employer, the approximate number of employees working for the employer, and a clear and concise statement of the alleged unlawful discrimination that includes pertinent dates.[4]

A federal judge in Florida ruled in 2015 that a plaintiff filed a timely charge when she filed an intake questionnaire with the EEOC.[5] He said the intake questionnaire indicated the plaintiff's intent to initiate the EEOC's administrative complaint process.

---

[3]*Federal Express Corp. v. Holowecki*, 552 U.S. 389 (2008). See also 29 C.F.R. § 1626.6.

[4] *Bost v. Fed. Express Corp.*, 372 F.3d 1233, 1238 (11th Cir. 2004) (citing 29 C.F.R. § 1626.8(a)(1)-(5))

[5] *Rodrigues v. SCM 1 Invs. LLC*, No. 2:15-cv-128-FtM-29CM (M.D. Fla. Nov. 2, 2015).

The Ticking Clock

A cause of action under the ADEA begins "on the date the employee is notified of an adverse employment decision."[6] This is when:

- A discriminatory employment decision or practice is adopted; or

- When a person is subject to a discriminatory decision or practice, including each time payment is made of wages, benefits or other compensation that are tainted by discriminatory decision or practice.[7]

In cases alleging a hostile work environment, the U.S. Supreme Court ruled in *National Railroad Passenger Corp. (Amtrak) v. Morgan*, 536 U.S. 101, (2002) that courts may consider allegations outside of the statute of limitations if at least one act contributing to the hostile work environment occurs during the filing period. This so-called "continuing violation doctrine" does not apply to claims of "discrete" discriminatory or retaliatory acts, which are time-barred if not filed within the statute of limitations.

---

[6] *Delaware State College v. Ricks*, 449 U.S. 250, 256-59 (1980).
[7] 29 U.S. Code § 626 (d) (3).

For complaints involving recurring discrimination, remember to check the "continuing violation" box on the EEOC's Charge of Discrimination.

Be aware that the EEOC's deadlines are not waived if an employee chooses to file a union grievance or internal complaint with the company. An EEOC complaint must be filed within the EEOC statute of limitations.

A Missed Deadline

There are limited circumstances where the EEOC or a federal court will accept a charge as timely even though it was not filed within the statute of limitations. The following exceptions are based upon the principal of equity or fairness:

- "Equitable tolling" is a form of forgiveness that is available if the charging party's lack of knowledge about the EEOC process or the alleged violation that caused the delay in filing is *excusable*. Equitable tolling may occur when a party had no reason to suspect discrimination; the complainant's mental state prevented him or her from pursuing legal remedies; or the complainant was given misinformation by the EEOC or a state field office.

- "Equitable estoppel" is intended to prevent an employer from benefitting from its own misconduct.

Estoppel is available if the employer inappropriately induced the charging party to delay filing an EEOC complaint by, for example, assuring the charging party that relief would be forthcoming through internal procedures. The filing period begins to run when the charging party knew or should have discovered the employer's misconduct.

- Waiver also is available if both parties agree to waive the filing period.

These equitable doctrines recognize the difficulties that workers face in discrimination cases. With respect to equitable tolling, an appeals court observed that "[s]ecret preferences in hiring and even more subtle means of illegal discrimination, because of their very nature, are unlikely to be readily apparent to the individual discriminated against."[8] Equitable tolling is intended to prevent a plaintiff from being unfairly precluded from pursuing justice because s/he was unaware of discrimination prior to the expiration of the statute of limitations.

Due Diligence

The filing period is only tolled until an individual has enough information to reasonably suspect that s/he has a

---

[8] *Reeb v. Economic Opportunity Atlanta, Inc.*, 516 F.2d 924, 931 (5th Cir. 1975).

valid discrimination claim. The filing period begins to run when workers realize they may have a claim even if they are not certain about the claim. And the complainant is expected to act with "due diligence" to obtain vital information.

A federal appeals court in 2015 reversed a lower court's denial of a job applicant request for equitable tolling of the 180-day statute of limitations in an ADEA lawsuit.[9] The appeals court ruled that a plaintiff is entitled to equitable tolling until "the facts supporting a cause of action become apparent or should have become apparent to a reasonably prudent person with concern for his or her rights."

In that case, Robert Villarreal, 49, got no response after he applied for a position as a territory manager at R.J. Reynolds Tobacco, Co., in 2007. He applied five more times and never got a response. Later, Villarreal learned that Reynolds used an internet-based resume screening tool that weeded out applications from older workers, and that only 19 of the 1,024 territory managers hired by Reynolds between 2007 and 2010 were over the age of 40. The appeals court noted that age discrimination is often hidden and so the clock should not start running on the statute of limitations until the plaintiff has enough information to support a cause of action.

---

[9] *Villarreal v. R.J. Reynolds Tobacco Co, Pinstripe, Inc. and CareerBuilder, L.L.C.,* No. 15-10602 (11th Cir., Nov. 30, 2015).

Too Late?

Linda, 56, applied for one of two vacancies at an accounting firm. On November 28, 2014, she received a letter stating she was not selected for a position. A month later, Linda learned that the successful candidates were both under age 30 and had far less experience. She suspected age discrimination.

Linda lived in a state with a Fair Employment Practices Agency and was required to file her age discrimination complaint within 300 days of the last discriminatory action. But Linda did not file her EEOC complaint until a month after the deadline expired.

Was she too late?

Linda could argue the deadline should be extended because she had no reason to suspect and did not suspect age discrimination until a month after she was denied the job.

But suppose Linda didn't file her complaint until several months after she suspected age discrimination? The EEOC or a court may elect not to toll the deadline unless Linda can show that the accounting firm was clearly responsible for the delay.

Victims of discrimination are expected to act with "due diligence."

◆

Federal courts generally are unsympathetic about missed deadlines. For example, an appeals court in 1990 refused to toll the EEOC's statute of limitations in a case where a plaintiff retired after being told that his position was being abolished. The plaintiff discovered more than a year later that he was replaced by a younger employee. "It is sufficient that [the complainant] was on notice at the moment of his alleged constructive termination 'to inquire whether there was [a] discriminatory motive for the discharge,'" ruled the court.

The U.S. Supreme Court in 2007 narrowly construed the statute of limitations for filing an EEOC charge in a famous case involving gender-based pay discrimination.[10] In *Ledbetter v. Goodyear*, the Court held that an employee was barred from filing an EEOC complaint alleging a Title VII violation because the claim was based on management decisions that occurred more than 180 days prior to the filing of the charge. The Court said a new violation does not occur - and a new charging period does not begin - each time

---

[10] *Ledbetter v. Goodyear*, 550 U.S. 618 (2007).

an employer issues a paycheck to a female employee that is less than what a similarly situated male employee receives.

Where to File

At this writing, complainants cannot file an EEOC complaint on-line. However, many state FEPAs permit on-line filing. A complaint filed with a FEPA is considered to have been filed with the EEOC. A complainant who wants to file a complaint directly with the EEOC can file by mail or in person at an EEOC office.

State FEPAs resolved 44,377 EEOC charges in Fiscal Year 2011.

For more information, contact the EEOC toll-free at 1-800-669-4000 or go to the agency's web site at www.eeoc.com.

➢ Intake

The EEOC intake process consists of a form of "triage" reminiscent of a hospital emergency room. Cases are diverted into one of three categories based upon how they fit within the EEOC's strategic plan and their perceived likelihood of success on the merits:

1. Category "A" cases include charges that fall within the EEOC's national or local enforcement plan or that are considered likely to lead to a finding that

discrimination occurred. These are high priority cases.

2. Category "B" cases are deemed by the EEOC to have potential importance but more evidence is needed to determine whether further investigation will result in a finding of cause.

3. The vast majority of charges default to Category "C." The EEOC concludes that it is unlikely that discrimination can be proven based on the evidence presented by the charging party. These charges are deemed "appropriate for immediate dismissal."

To lower the chance of ending up in the dead end of Category "C," complainant would be wise to go beyond making mere allegations in their EEOC charge. Ideally, a charge should set forth persuasive evidence of discrimination and a showing that it caused or will cause serious harm to the complainant and others. It also wouldn't hurt emphasize any connection between the alleged discrimination and the EEOC's national strategic plan.

The EEOC in 2012 adopted a strategic plan that established the following priorities:

- Eliminating barriers in recruitment and hiring;
- Protecting immigrant, migrant and other vulnerable workers;

- Addressing emerging and developing issues;

- Enforcing equal pay laws;

- Preserving access to the legal system;

- Preventing harassment through systemic enforcement and targeted outreach.

Roll the Dice?

The EEOC has been criticized for failing to insure consistency between its offices around the country. The Office of the Inspector General (OIG), an independent agency that oversees the EEOC and other federal agencies, issued a report in 2013 urging the EEOC to adopt uniform and standardized intake procedures "across field offices." The OIG said the change was needed to "improve consistency in charge categorization."

The OIG pointed to several variables that can influence how a charge is handled. For example, the OIG said that charge assessments are influenced by staff shortages or when a field office is inundated with charges. A charge may be deemed more or less significant depending upon how it is presented to the EEOC. Staff may perceive a charge prepared by an attorney to be more importantt than one prepared by the complainant.

Many complainants are at a disadvantage when drafting their EEOC complaint because they lack access to key facts, which are known only to the employer. For example, older job applicants may strongly suspect age discrimination in hiring but they generally don't know the ages and qualifications of the other candidates. As a result, their charge may appear to be conclusory. An EEOC investigation would elicit the facts through witness statements, depositions and subpoenas. However, there will be no EEOC investigation if a charge is dumped into Category "C" and dismissed at the intake stage.

Many valid cases of age discrimination are dismissed by the EEOC for seemingly arbitrary reasons. For example, the EEOC announced in 2012 that it would focus more in the future on systemic discrimination or discrimination resulting from a practice or policy that has a broad impact upon an industry, occupation or geographic area. The increased focus on systemic discrimination will invariably shift resources away from individual complaints. Thus, individual complaints that the EEOC might pursued in the past will labelled Category "C." Twenty five percent of the 228 of the cases on the EEOC's litigation docket in 2014 involved systemic discrimination.

The vast majority of age discrimination charges filed with the EEOC go nowhere. The EEOC operates like a temporary holding pen. Charges are reviewed, categorized and, after six months, the complainant is sent a "Right to Sue" letter.

According to a 2008 study by the American Bar Foundation, the EEOC failed to "make a finding or non-finding of reasonable cause" in nearly 77 percent of all discrimination complaints from 1987 to 2003.[11] The EEOC intervened as a plaintiff in only three percent of all employment discrimination charges.

> *"[T]he EEOC does not typically get very far through the administrative process, and only rarely does the EEOC side with the complainant." – American Bar Foundation*

After receiving a "Right to Sue" letter, the complainant has 90 days to file an age discrimination lawsuit in federal court.

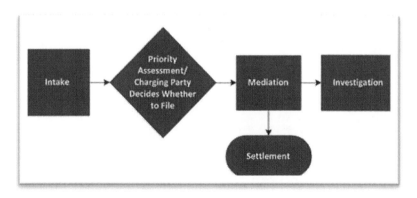

---

[11] Nielsen, L.B., et. al, *Contesting Workplace Discrimination in Court; Characteristics and Outcomes of Federal Employment Litigation (1987-2003)*, 14, The American Bar Foundation (October 29, 2008).

➤ Mediation

Mediation is a form of free, confidential and voluntary dispute resolution that is offered by the EEOC as an alternative to its traditional investigative and litigation process. The EEOC does not offer mediation if it determines a case is "without merit."

In the past, mediation took place before the EEOC's investigated a charge of discrimination. However, the EEOC has expanded the program in recent years to make mediation available when an EEOC investigation has resulted in a finding of discrimination.

In mediation, a neutral mediator assists the employer and employee in reaching a voluntary resolution of the employment dispute. The mediator may be an EEOC staff member or an independent contractor. The mediator and the parties must sign agreements that they will keep everything that is revealed during the mediation confidential. The process, which is not tape-recorded or transcribed, typically takes four or five hours.

If one party does not agree to a settlement, the charge is transferred to the EEOC's investigative unit or the complainant is issued a "right to sue" letter.

In cases where the EEOC already has found reasonable cause to believe the employer engaged in age discrimination, an EEOC staff member sits in as a participant in the mediation, along with the charging party, respondent and mediator. If the mediation is not successful, the EEOC retains the option of filing its own lawsuit against the employer.

Mediation is almost always beneficial for employers because it is free, completely secret and, at worst, gives the employer a snapshot of the worker's evidence. Mediation gives the employer a chance to avoid attorney fees, the risk of bad publicity and a costly damages award. The benefits rise exponentially if mediation takes place *after* an EEOC investigation has determined there is reasonable cause to believe that discrimination occurred.

Mediation is a great deal for employers, who obtain cost-free dispute resolution and avoid the risk of a lawsuit. Not so much for age discrimination victims.

Mediation presents a much more complicated picture for victims of age discrimination.

Employers generally are represented by an experienced employment law attorney. Most age discrimination charges are filed by older workers who lost their jobs. They can't afford to retain an attorney and subsidize three-to five-years of litigation. Workers who must represent themselves may have little understanding of the law (let alone the complex morass of age discrimination law). Moreover, workers often come into the process of mediation emotionally and devastated; many are not capable of being zealous and effective advocates of their own best interests.

> *Mediation traditionally has not been recommended in cases that involve severe emotional abuse, such as domestic violence cases, because victims may be in fear of or intimidated by the perpetrator of the abuse. They cannot effectively advocate for their best interests. Similarly, mediation may not be appropriate in age discrimination cases that involve severe emotional abuse, such as when a manager harasses an older worker to force him or her to retire.*

In the context of an employment discrimination case, what you don't know can hurt you. Prior to an EEOC investigation, the complainant may not have all of the facts (and will never get them if mediation is successful). Complainants may not understand that an EEOC investigator could obtain critical evidence from the employer. Complainants may accept a minimal settlement without realizing they actually have a very strong case and the potential to collect significant damages. Employers, of course, know this.

> *For the complainant, accepting a settlement can be like purchasing a used car without inspecting what is under the hood.*

Another downside to mediation for the victim of age discrimination is that a successful mediation typically produces a very modest settlement that does not come close to adequately compensating older workers who have suffered real and lasting damage. Age discrimination plaintiffs almost never get what they want the most - their jobs back.

The EEOC states that its private sector mediation program in 2014 achieved a resolution in 7,846 mediations out of a total of 10,221 mediations conducted for all types of discrimination. The EEOC states its mediation effort secured a total of $144.6 million in monetary benefits for complainants, which amounts to about $18,430 per mediation. This is paltry recompense for older workers who lost jobs or were not hired due to illegal age discrimination.

Despite the downside for victims of age discrimination, the EEOC maintains that over 96 percent of participants reported confidence in the mediation program in 2014.[12]

---

[12] Statement of Jenny R. Yang, Chair of the U.S. Equal Employment Opportunity Commission, before the U.S. Senate Committee on Health, Education, Labor and Pensions (May 19, 2015), retrieved on 11/29/2015 from http://www.eeoc.gov/eeoc/legislative/yang_5-19-15.cfm

It is not hard to believe that mediation is an attractive option. Most age discrimination victims cannot afford to subsidize years of federal litigation. Furthermore, workers may fear that any publicity about their case will brand them a "troublemaker" and doom their future job prospects. Many complainants lack the emotional wherewithal to fight. Moreover, it may seem as if the victim has little to lose. The clock stops while the EEOC seeks "voluntary compliance ... but in no event for a period in excess of one year."[13] So the complainant can still file a lawsuit if mediation fails.

In reality, however, unsuccessful mediation can be a crushing final blow to an older worker who already has suffered so much. Many complainants simply give up on valid claims in the aftermath of an unsuccessful mediation. After enduring the trauma of age discrimination, they don't have the stomach for America's brutal and unsympathetic federal court system.

An agreement reached pursuant to mediation, like any other settlement agreement, is enforceable by the court.

➤ Investigation

The EEOC is required to "develop an impartial and appropriate factual record upon which to make findings on the claims raised by the written complaint." The EEOC has

---

[13] 29 U.S.C. 6262 (e) (2).

broad authority and many investigatory tools, including subpoena power.

An Equal Employment Opportunity investigator may visit the employer to hold interviews and gather documents or can opt to interview witnesses over the phone and request documents by mail. Occasionally, the EEOC will expand its investigation to include evidence of unlawful employment practices against other employees when it is relevant to a charge under investigation.

The EEOC investigator develops the factual record but does not decide the merits of the case.

The investigator does not reach a conclusion as to whether discrimination occurred but rather develops an evidentiary record. Statements and evidence produced in the investigation are admissible as evidence in an administrative or court hearing.

Complainants are required to cooperate with the investigation and to keep the agency informed of their current address. If a complainant fails to respond to a written request by the agency for information, the complaint can be dismissed. According to the EEOC, the average investigation takes about six months.

Tip! An issue of confidentiality may arise if the plaintiff's mental state becomes an issue. An employer may demand to see the psychological reports, including therapist notes, of a worker who states that s/he sought psychological counseling as a result of an employer's discriminatory treatment.

At the end of an investigation, the EEOC determines whether it is likely that a violation of the law occurred. If the EEOC determines there is reasonable cause to believe that discrimination occurred, the parties may be issued a letter inviting them to settle the case through mediation or conciliation, an informal and confidential process of dispute resolution. If not, the EEOC may decide to sue the employer (though this rarely happens). When the EEOC finds it is not likely the ADEA was violated, the complainant is sent a letter called a "Dismissal and Notice of Rights." The letter advises complainants that they have a right to file a lawsuit in federal or state court within 90 days of receipt of the letter. The employer is sent a copy of the letter.

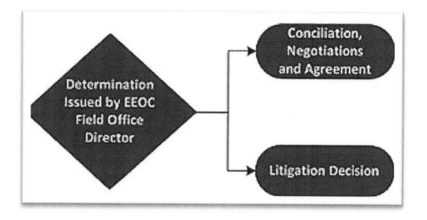

➢ **Conciliation**

If the EEOC concludes there is reasonable cause to believe that discrimination occurred, the agency is required to endeavor "to eliminate any such alleged unlawful employment practice by informal methods of conference, conciliation, and persuasion."[14] This process is known as conciliation. The EEOC works with the employee and the employer to resolve the charge of discrimination and to eliminate future unlawful employment practices. If a satisfactory resolution is achieved through conciliation, the EEOC and the employee agree not to file a lawsuit against the employer. If conciliation is unsuccessful, the EEOC can either bring a lawsuit on behalf of the employee or release the matter to the individual to file a lawsuit independently.

---

[14] 42 U.S.C. § 2000e-5(b).

The EEOC states that conciliation is becoming increasingly popular with employers. The EEOC notes that it improved its rate of successful conciliations from 27 percent in 2010 to 38 percent in 2014. According to the EEOC, "This means that more and more often employers are coming to the table after an investigation and resolving more complaints with conciliation agreements, without the need for protracted litigation."

The EEOC conciliated four systemic ADEA investigations in 2014 in which employers agreed to stop prohibiting volunteer firefighters from accruing points for performing certain duties when they reached age 55 or 60. The EEOC states the volunteer firefighters received more than $1.4 million and the employers changed their policies to bring them into compliance with the ADEA.

The EEOC offers discriminatory employers a chance to voluntarily comply with the ADEA in the future in exchange for a promise not to sue.

In recent years, the EEOC came under pressure to be more conciliatory and less hard-nosed in the conciliation process. Employers charged the EEOC was making it too difficult to resolve discrimination charges through conciliation. The U.S. Supreme Court, of course, agreed with the employers. The Court ruled in 2015 that the EEOC must tell employers which of its practices harmed the complainant and to "provide the employer with the opportunity to discuss the matter in an effort to achieve voluntary compliance." In most instances, the Court said, the EEOC can meet this obligation by submitting an affidavit to the court outlining its offer of conciliation. However, the Court said an employer can dispute the EEOC's affidavit and request a hearing.[15] From an age discrimination victim's perspective, the Court's ruling offers discriminatory employers yet another opportunity to forestall accountability for their illegal actions and lower a potential monetary award.

In addition to monetary damages, the EEOC can demand a range of concessions in its conciliation offer, such completion of training programs and an agreement to undergo EEOC monitoring for a period of time.

When the EEOC files an ADEA action, it terminates the claimant's right to file a private lawsuit in the matter.

When conciliation efforts fail, the EEOC can pursue litigation, though it seldom does. In fiscal year 2014, the EEOC filed a total of 167 lawsuits, of which 12 contained age discrimination claims. That year, the EEOC received 88,778 charges, including 20,588 age discrimination complaints.

---

[15] *Mach Mining, LLC V. Equal Employment Opportunity Commission*, No. 13-1019, decided April 29, 2015.

➤ **Right to Sue**

A "Right to Sue" letter from the EEOC sounds the death knell for most age discrimination complaints. The EEOC has closed the case. After receiving the letter, complainants must file a court action within 90 days or they forever lose their right to sue.[16]

Unfortunately, a "Right to Sue" does not translate into an ability to sue- especially for older workers who lost their jobs or were not hired due to age discrimination. Many attorneys require a five figure advance to take an age discrimination case. Some attorneys won't take the case at all unless the victim earned a hefty salary because the potential damages are considered too low to justify the effort. Without a source of income, it is difficult for the victim to finance years of federal litigation and many victims cannot or don't want to represent themselves in a federal court lawsuit.

The ADEA was amended in 1978 to provide the plaintiff with a right to a jury trial.[17]

---

[16] 29 U.S. Code § 626 (e).
[17] 29 U.S.C. 626 (c).

9. ARBITRATION

The U.S. Supreme Court has ruled that nothing in the language of the ADEA or its legislative history precludes arbitration.[1] As a result, a compulsory arbitration clause signed by an employee or contained in an employer handbook that is provided to the employee can quickly derail an ADEA lawsuit.

The ADEA emphasizes informal methods of dispute resolution, such as conciliation and persuasion –
U.S. Supreme Court

Robert D. Gilmer, 62, was a manager of financial services at Interstate/Johnson Lane Corp. who was fired in 1987. When he was hired in 1981, his employer required him to sign a registration application with the New York Stock Exchange in which he agreed to arbitrate any claim or dispute with Interstate. After Gilmer filed an age discrimination lawsuit, Interstate argued that Gilmer was barred from going to court by the arbitration clause in his employment application. The U.S. Supreme Court agreed. The Court said Gilmer failed to show that Congress intended to preclude

---

[1] *Gilmer v. Interstate/Johnson Lane Corp*, 500 US 20 (1991).

arbitration in statutory claims (such as an ADEA claim) when it passed the Federal Arbitration Act (FAA) of 1925.

However, courts will look closely at arbitration clauses to insure that they are fair and enforceable. A Missouri court in 2015 rejected an arbitration clause that allowed the employer to unilaterally and retroactively modify an arbitration agreement.[2]

➤ Union Contracts

The U.S. Supreme Court issued a controversial 5-to-4 decision in 2009 stating that a union can waive the rights of its members to file an ADEA lawsuit even if the union members did not agree to the waiver.[3]

The Court ruled in *14 Penn Plaza, LLC, v. Pyett* that a collectively bargained mandatory arbitration agreement that covers claims of employment discrimination is enforceable. However, the Court stressed, the bargaining agreement must "clearly and unmistakably" require arbitration of such claims. The majority held that an arbitration clause in a union contract does not take away members' substantive rights; it simply requires that the forum for the enforcement of those rights be transferred from the courts to an arbitrator.

---

[2] *Baker v. Bristol Care, Inc.,* 450 SW 3d 770 (2014).
[3] *14 Penn Plaza LLC v. Pyett*, 556 U.S. 247 (2009)

A contract clause waiving a union member's right to go to court must be specific and unambiguous.

In a dissent, Justice John Paul Stevens said the majority's ruling flew in the face of an earlier unanimous Court ruling[4] that expressed concern about entrusting a union with certain arbitration decisions "given the potential conflict between the collective interest and the interests of an individual employee seeking to assert his rights."

Justice Steven expressed doubt that Congress in 1925 anticipated the Federal Arbitration Act would ever be applied to statutory claims "to form contracts between parties of unequal bargaining power, or to the arbitration of disputes arising out of the employment relationship." He said the Court had effectively re-written the FAA.

Justice Clarence Thomas, who wrote the majority decision, said the majority was correcting the Court's "mistaken suggestion" in the earlier case that arbitration is not an appropriate forum.

To be effective, a union-negotiated waiver of employees' right to sue for employment discrimination must be unambiguously set forth in a collective bargaining agreement. A general arbitration statement in a grievance procedure clause is not sufficient.[5]

---

[4] *Alexander v. Gardner–Denver Co.*, 415 U.S. 36 (1974)
[5] *Wright v. Universal Maritime Service Corp.*, 525 U.S. 70 (1998).

The EEOC is Free to Sue

If an employee is subject to an arbitration clause, the EEOC is not. The EEOC can file an age discrimination lawsuit even if union members do not have a right to sue, though it rarely does. The EEOC is deemed to be filing suit in the public's interest, not just the individual worker.

The EEOC represents the public's interest.

The U.S. Supreme Court in a 6-3 ruling in 2002 held that the EEOC could not be bound by a contract to which it was not a party. The Court said the EEOC could pursue a disability charge in a case in which a restaurant grill operator in South Carolina was fired after having a seizure at work. The grill operator had signed an employment contract containing a compulsory arbitration clause.

Justice John Paul Stevens, writing for the majority, said the EEOC has the authority, whenever a complaint is filed with the agency, to "evaluate the strength of the public interest at stake and to determine whether public resources should be committed to the recovery of victim-specific relief." The Court concluded the EEOC has exclusive authority over the choice of forum for addressing the complaint.

10. DISPARATE TREATMENT (INTENTIONAL DISCRIMINATION)

> "Employers are rarely so cooperative as to include a notation in the personnel file, "fired due to age," or to inform a dismissed employee candidly that he is too old for the job."
>
> - From *Thornbrough v. Columbia & Greenville R.R. Co.*, 760 F.2d 633, n. 14 (5th Cir. 1985).

The vast majority of age discrimination complaints filed with the EEOC involve intentional discrimination, also known as disparate treatment discrimination. An example of disparate treatment discrimination is when an employer fires an older worker and replaces him or her with a younger employee to project a more youthful image for the company.

> *"The ultimate question in every disparate treatment case is whether the plaintiff was the victim of intentional discrimination."- U.S. Supreme Court*[1]

In a disparate treatment case, the plaintiff must show the employer intended to discriminate. It is not enough to show that age was merely a factor in an adverse employment action. The U.S. Supreme Court ruled in 1999 that it is not

---

[1] *Reeves v Sanderson Plumbing Products*, 530 U.S. 133 (2000).

"intentional discrimination" when an employer bases a decision to terminate an employee on a permissible factor that is "highly correlated" with age.[2] For example, the Court has ruled that it is not age discrimination if an employer is motivated by cost savings or seeks to prevent an older worker from vesting in the company's pension fund.

'Because of' Age

Walter F. Biggins, 62, had worked at a paper manufacturing company for almost ten years. He was dismissed a few months before he was scheduled to vest in the company's pension plan.

The U.S. Supreme Court unanimously ruled in 1993 that the company dismissed Biggins to prevent him from vesting in the pension plan and not because of his age discrimination.

Justice Sandra Day O'Connor, who wrote the decision, said a plaintiff in an age discrimination case must prove that age "actually motivated the employer's decision." She said pension status and years of service are "analytically distinct" because an employer can "take into account of one while

---

[2] . See *Hazen Paper Co. v. Biggins*, 507 U.S. 604, 611 (1993).

ignoring the other." Moreover, Justice O'Connor said Congress enacted the ADEA to eliminate prohibited stereotypes and that Higgin's dismissal was not based upon a prohibited stereotype.[3]

◆

In addition to showing intent to discriminate, the plaintiff must demonstrate the employer deprived or tended to deprive the employee of "employment opportunities or otherwise adversely affect his status as an employee."[4] An unfair warning or performance evaluation may not rise to a level of harm that triggers protection under the ADEA. Also, to be eligible for monetary damages, ADEA plaintiffs must show they suffered economic loss. Unlike Title VII, the ADEA does not provide damages for compensatory damages (e.g. emotional distress) or punitive damages.

Causation

Age discrimination plaintiffs must also show a causal connection between age discrimination and the adverse employment action (i.e. demotion, dismissal). The plaintiff must show that "but for" age discrimination, the adverse

---

[3] But see *Tramp v. Associated Underwriters, Inc.*, 2012 WL 4977396 (8th Cir. 2014). The appeals court said an employer can violate the ADEA by terminating an older employee to reduce health care premiums. The court said health care costs could be a proxy for age and, regardless of whether age and health care costs are in fact analytically distinct, there was an issue of fact as to whether Defendant fired the plaintiff for age-related reasons.
[4] See *Smith v. City of Jackson*, 544 U.S. 228, 250 (U.S. 2005).

action would not have occurred. In other words, age discrimination must be the determining factor and not simply a motivating factor. A minority of federal courts require plaintiffs to show that age discrimination was the *only* reason for the adverse employment action.

➤ Elements of Disparate Treatment

To prove intentional or disparate treatment age discrimination, plaintiffs must show they:

- Suffered an adverse action. An adverse employment action has been defined as a "materially adverse change in the terms and conditions of a plaintiff's employment." [5] This can take many forms, from a reassignment that constitutes a demotion to termination.

- Were age 40 or above when the adverse action occurred; and

- The employer would not have subjected them to the adverse action "but for" their age. In other words, age discrimination was the determinative influence on the outcome or adverse action.

* *See* Chapter 18, Retaliation, for additional discussion of adverse action.

---

[5] *White v. Burlington N. & Santa Fe Ry. Co.*, 364 F.3d 789, 795 (6th Cir. 2004)

The Empty Page

The hiring officer made marks and notations on the resumes of job applicants who were under the age of 40 but there were no marks on the resumes of applicants who were aged 40 and above. This indicates that he failed to consider qualified older applicants for the job vacancy, which is evidence of discrimination.[6]

◆

➤ Bona Fide Occupational Qualification

The ADEA contains an "escape clause" that allows employers to engage in age discrimination when age is a "bona fide occupational qualification" (BFOQ) that is "reasonably" necessary to the normal operation of the particular business.[7] Thus, an employer can defend itself against a charge of age discrimination by showing that its consideration of age was reasonable and necessary. It is considered to be a bona fide occupational qualification, for example, to hire a teenager for a job that involves modeling

---

[6] (See *Johnson v. Maestri-Murrell Prop. Mgmt.*, LLC, 487 F. App'x 134, 135 (5th Cir. 2012)).
[7] 29 U.S.C. § 623(f).

clothing for teenagers. It is not a BFOQ to require all servers in a restaurant to be under the age of 40.

Elements of a BFOQ Defense

To qualify as a BFOQ defense under the ADEA, the EEOC requires that an employer prove:

- ✓ The age limit was reasonably necessary to the essence of the business;
- ✓ All or substantially all individuals excluded from the job involved are in fact disqualified; or,
- ✓ Some of the individuals who were excluded possess a disqualifying trait that cannot be ascertained except by reference to age.[8]

For a supposedly 'narrow' exception, the BFOQ defense covers a lot of ground..

The U.S. Supreme Court has ruled that the BFOQ is "an extremely narrow exception to the general prohibition of age discrimination contained in the ADEA."[9] The EEOC maintains that the BFOQ defense is "limited scope and applications" and should be "narrowly construed." In reality, a broad range of occupations, from bus drivers to airline pilots, are or have been subject to age-related BFOQs.

---

[8] 29 C.F.R. § 1625.6(b) (2006).
[9] *Western Airlines v. Criswell*, 472 U.S. 400, 412 (1985).

The BFOQ defense can be based upon an arbitrary age having no scientific foundation. For example, the U.S. Office of Personnel Management requires U.S. border patrol agents to be "younger than 37 at the time of selection" unless the applicant is a veteran, in which case the requirement is waived. There is no evidence that a 38-year-old is less capable of performing the duties of a border patrol agent. And if the age limit is important enough to impose in the first place, why is it waived because the applicant served in the military? It would be one thing if a veteran had relevant skills but the exception also applies to veterans who were cooks, file room clerks, and drivers. The seemingly random BFOQ has the effect of discriminating against older workers who are perfectly fit to perform the job.

Technically, the U.S. Supreme Court has stated that a general concern is not sufficient to justify a safety-based BFOQ. An employer must demonstrate beyond a mere "rational basis" why a particular job qualification cannot be determined on an individualized basis.[10] The Court said a BFOQ must be based on "the likelihood of harm and the probable severity of harm." A BFOQ also must be reasonably necessary to the "essence" of the business.[11]

---

[10] Id. at 417-23.
[11] *Id.* at 413.

The EEOC goes even farther than the nation's high court in narrowly defining a safety-based BFOQ. The EEOC requires employers to prove that the BFOQ furthers public safety and "there is no acceptable alternative which would advance it better advance it or equally advance it with less discriminatory impact." Of course, EEOC regulations are not binding on the courts.

'Essence' of a Business

As noted above, the U.S. Supreme Court says a BFOQ must be "reasonably necessary" to the essence of the business or profession.

Courts have upheld fire department tests that require job applicants to carry heavy weights, even though this requirement disproportionately excludes women, the disabled and older applicants. A firefighter must hoist heavy hoses and ladders and carry unconscious individuals from a burning building. It is reasonably necessary to the essence of the business of a firefighter to carry heavy weights. However, employers often impose requirements that are not reasonable or necessary to the essence of a business.

A federal appeals court ruled, for example, that it is not reasonable for a restaurant chain to hire only male servers to create an atmosphere of old world formality.[12] The court said the essence of the business of a restaurant is to serve food. Similarly, the EEOC has sued restaurant chains that refuse to hire older workers for "front of the house" jobs, such as host or server.

Note: an employer cannot require only older applicants to take a physical agility test, based upon a belief that they are less physically able to perform a particular job. All applicants must be tested.

♦

Higher Standard

There also is a BFOQ clause in Title VII of the Civil Rights Act, which prohibits discrimination based on race, sex, religion, color, and national origin. Title VII requires an employer to show that discrimination is a "business necessity" and there is no less discriminatory alternative. This standard is much stricter than the ADEA's requirement that a BFOQ must be "reasonably" necessary to the normal operation of the business.

---

[12] *EEOC v. Joe's Stone Crab, Inc.*, 220 F. 3d 1263 (11th Cir. 2000).

There is, of course, no legitimate justification for legalizing baseless employment discrimination against older workers when the same conduct would be illegal if it were directed at another protected class.

Burden of Proof

Under the ADEA, plaintiffs must prove age discrimination by a *preponderance of the evidence*. This means that plaintiffs must show their version of the facts is more likely than not the correct version. This burden is meant to be light and requires the plaintiff to show only that the scale of justice is tipped in the plaintiff's favor.

An Avalanche of Dismissals

Employers who are defendants in ADEA lawsuits typically file a motion for summary judgment, at the earliest stage to avoid costly discovery. The employer argues the case should be dismissed as a matter of law because no genuine issue of any material fact is in dispute.[13]

One study found that 73 percent of employment discrimination cases are dismissed by federal judges

---

[13] *See* Title VII, Judgment. Rule 56, Federal Rules of Civil Procedure.

119

on motions for summary judgment.[14] There is a much higher rate of dismissal in employment cases than in other business litigation. For example, only 53 percent of contract cases are dismissed on a motion for summary judgment.

One former federal judge has accused other federal judges of essentially "interpreting" discrimination laws out of existence.[15]

For decades, a pleading could not be dismissed "unless it appears beyond doubt that the plaintiff can prove no set of facts in support of his claim."[16] This changed in 2009 when U.S. Supreme Court ruled that judges may use their own "judicial experience and common sense" to determine whether claimants have set forth facts sufficient to "nudge their claims across the line from conceivable to plausible."[17]

♦

---

[14] Joe Cecil & George Cort, Federal Judicial Center, *Estimates of Summary Judgment Activity in Fiscal Year 2006* (2007).

[15] Nancy Gertner, Losers' Rules, 122 Yale L.J. Online 109 (2012), http://yalelawjournal.org/forum/losers-rules.

[16] *Conley v. Gibson*, 355 U.S. 41, 45–46 (1957).

[17] *Ashcroft v. Iqbal*, 556 U.S. 662 (2009). See also *Bell Atlantic v. Twombly*, 550 U.S. 544 (2007).

➢ Discovery

Discovery is a process in which parties to a lawsuit ask each other for information about the case. There are several types of discovery, including:

- **Request for Interrogatories**: One party asks the other to provide answers to a set of written questions.

- **Request for Documents**: This is a request that one side submits to the other for written or electronic information that is relevant to the case. For example, a plaintiff in a hiring discrimination case might ask the employer to turn over any notes taken during the interview stage.

- **Request for Admissions**: One party asks the other to admit or deny a series of questions or factual statements. For example, the plaintiff might ask: "Did the interviewer ask all of the job applicants the same questions?" The defendant can say "yes" or "no," "admit in part and deny in part" or state that it does not know the answer.

- **Depositions**: At a deposition, one side questions parties or witnesses for the other side. The normal rules of evidence do not apply. A court reporter records the exchange, which may be videotaped. Each party must pay its own costs if they wish to purchase a copy of the deposition testimony. Generally, a judge is available via the telephone to resolve any disputes between the parties.

➤ Evidence

Evidence is, for many, like beauty. It is subjective and hard to define. It is in the eye of the beholder. However, evidence is subject to strict rules in the court system. There, evidence must be relevant. Under Rule 401 of the Federal Rules of Evidence relevant evidence is "evidence having any tendency to make the existence of any fact that is of consequence to the determination of the action more probable or less probable than it would be without the evidence." For example, it is not relevant if a business owner accused of age discrimination sent his mother a Mother's Day card. This fact does not shed light on whether the business owner engaged in age discrimination. It's not relevant. It is generally not relevant when a witness testifies about what s/he heard another person say- that's hearsay.

There are generally two types of evidence, direct evidence and indirect evidence.

1. Direct Evidence

Direct evidence is evidence that needs no other explanation. It shows the existence of discrimination on its face. Plaintiffs with direct evidence are not required to resort to the complicated burden-shifting formula that is mandated when a case depends upon inference or circumstantial evidence. Theoretically, direct evidence of age discrimination can lead to an automatic finding of discrimination against an employer.

The U.S. Supreme Court ruled in a 1989 that a plaintiff who produces direct evidence showing that an employer used "illegitimate criterion" when making an employment decision meets their burden of proof by that evidence alone.[18]

Examples of direct evidence include:

- A statement by a hiring officer, such as, "This job isn't right for you. You're too old."

- An email in which a company owner tells a manager to fire a 50-year-old receptionist because she sounds old on the telephone.

- A manager repeatedly encourages an older worker to retire, even after the worker said he has no wish to retire.

Direct evidence is the most persuasive kind of evidence because it needs no explanation. It is self-evident.

---

[18] *Price Waterhouse v. Hopkins,* 490 U.S. 228 (1989)

A $26.1 Million Bell Pepper

One of the largest jury awards in an age discrimination case involved an older worker who was fired because he allegedly stole a 68 cent bell pepper.

Bobby Dean Nickel, 64, a facilities manager at a Staples warehouse in Los Angeles, CA, was regularly referred to as "old coot" and "old goat" at staff meetings.

Nickel was fired in 2012 after refusing to resign, despite nine years of positive employment reviews. Nickel said Staples wanted to replace him with a lower-paid younger worker so it engaged in a campaign of false accusations and harassment. At one point, Nickel said his manager remarked, in front of HR personnel, "Take a closer look at the older people. They are starting to drag and are slowing down. If they are not top performers, write them up and get rid of them."

Nickel ultimately was suspended for taking a bell pepper worth 68 cents from the employee cafeteria.

The jury didn't buy Staples' defense that taking a bell pepper violated Staples' 'zero tolerance' honesty policy.

Nickel introduced the manager's comments as evidence, plus testimony from a receptionist who said she was ordered by management to provide a false statement about Nickel's conduct.

The Los Angeles, CA, Superior Court jury deliberated for four hours before finding in Nickel's favor on both his state law age discrimination claim and a claim of wrongful termination.

Nickel was awarded $3.2 million in compensatory damages and $22.8 million in punitive damages.

◆

2. Indirect Evidence

Employers today are too savvy to provide older workers with a neat bundle of direct evidence to prove age discrimination. Modern-day age discrimination often is subtle and hidden. For example, employers often argue that older workers are fired for performance-based reasons. Or they cite a list of subjective reasons that are difficult to disprove (i.e. less enthusiastic than younger workers during the job interview).

Without direct evidence, the task of proving age discrimination can be difficult. Plaintiffs must construct a *prima facie* ("at first appearance") case using circumstantial evidence to avoid pre-trial dismissal.

The U.S. Supreme Court in 1973 announced a formula that plaintiffs must use to prove a prima facie case of discrimination using indirect evidence. [19] It is known as the McDonnell Douglas burden shifting formula. The formula varies depending upon the type of discrimination (i.e., race, sex or age) involved and the type of an adverse employment action involved (i.e., demotion, termination, failure to hire). In an ADEA, the formula goes something like this:

1.   Plaintiffs must demonstrate they were:
     - Members of the protected class (age 40 or older);
     - Qualified for the position in question or working in a satisfactory manner.
     - Suffered an adverse employment decision (i.e. fired, demoted, not hired, not given a raise) because of their age; and,
     - They were treated less favorably than someone who is not in the protected class (i.e., under age 40) in terms of pay, promotion, retention, etc.
2.   If the plaintiff succeeds, a presumption arises that the employer engaged in unlawful age discrimination. The

---

[19] *McDonnell Douglas Corp. v. Green*, 411 U.S. 792 (1973).

defendant must articulate a legitimate non-discriminatory reason for the adverse employment action. The employer does not have to prove that the stated reason was the actual reason.[20]

3. The burden returns to the plaintiff to show that the employer's stated reason is a pretext for discrimination. The plaintiff must show the employer's stated reason is factually incorrect or that it is not the true reason for the challenged action but was offered to hide illegal age discrimination.

DISPARATE TREATMENT

- Employee aged 40+ suffered adverse employment action (i.e., demoted, fired).
- Employee was doing his/her job satisfactorily or job applicant was qualified for hire.
- Individuals who were not aged 40+ were treated more favorably.

Defense

- Bona Fide Occupational Qualification (BFOQ).
- Must be reasonably necessary to the normal operation of the business.

---

[20] *Gross v. FBL Fin. Servs., Inc.*, 129 S. Ct. 2343, 2351 (2009). The burden of proof never shifts from the plaintiff.

➢ **Pretext**

To determine whether the employer's stated non-discriminatory reason is a pretext for age discrimination, fact-finders must weigh conflicting testimony and evidence.

Courts look skeptically upon employers that are caught in a lie or that shift from one reason to another to explain an adverse employment action.

> *Pretext = Employer's reason was offered to hide illegal age discrimination.*

An employer's departure from its typical policies and practices may also be considered evidence of pretext. For example, many employers offer their employees a progressive disciplinary plan with distinct steps that lead to termination. It is telling when employers do not follow their own policies and procedures.[21]

One appellate court concluded that sufficient evidence of pretext is produced by showing "such weaknesses, implausibilities, inconsistencies, incoherencies, or contradictions in the employer's proffered legitimate reasons for its action that a reasonable factfinder could rationally find them unworthy of credence and hence infer that the

---

[21] *Goudeau v. National Oilwell Varco, LP*, No. 14-20241 (5th Cir. July 16, 2015).

employer did not act for the asserted non-discriminatory reasons."[22]

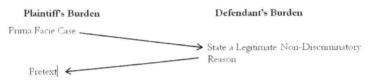

MCDONNELL DOUGLAS BURDEN SHIFTING FORMULA

Plaintiff's Burden   Defendant's Burden

Prima Facie Case

State a Legitimate Non-Discriminatory Reason

Pretext

Indirect or circumstantial evidence may include statistical evidence, evidence of harassment, discriminatory statements, co-worker discrimination, etc.

A federal court judge in Connecticut upheld a finding of intentional discrimination in a 2000 case where there was a revealing lack of any evidence. The plaintiff's evidence was limited to a statistical analysis.[23] The court noted the employer, United Technologies Corp. executed a layoff through a "highly unusual process that employed no written instructions or criterion and lacked any documentation." As a result, the court observed, the plaintiffs had no way to prove the selection process was biased except through statistical evidence.

---

[22] See *Jones v. Oklahoma City Public Schools*, 617 F.3d 1273, 1280 (10th Cir. 2010), *quoting Jaramillo v. Colorado Judicial Dept.*, 427 F.3d 1303, 1308 (10th Cir. 2005).

[23] *Schanzer v. United Technologies Corp.*, 120 F.Supp.2d 200 (D.Conn. 2000).

Confusion

To many both inside and outside the legal profession, the McDonnell Douglas burden shifting formula is a confusing ping-pong match. Some judges are loath to even read juries instructions setting forth the McDonnell Douglass formula prior to their deliberations for fear of hopelessly derailing them before they even start. "[T]o read [the McDonnell Douglas test's] technical aspects to a jury . . . will add little to the juror's understanding of the case and, even worse, may lead jurors to abandon their own judgment and to seize upon poorly understood legalisms to decide the ultimate question of discrimination," wrote one judge.[24] Moreover, when there are several different claims in a case, such as a promotion claim, a salary claim, and a termination claim, "the parties and the court would have to go through the eight steps for each claim."[25]

---

[24] *Loeb v. Textron, Inc.,* 600 F.2d 1003, 1016 (1st Cir. 1979).
[25] Hon. Denny Chin, *Summary Judgment in Employment Discrimination Cases: A Judge's Perspective,* 57 N.Y.L. Sch. L. Rev. 671, 678 (2012-2013).

Plaintiffs who are forced to represent themselves are faced with the challenge of mastering a formula of proof that is acknowledged to baffle the average juror. All any self-represented litigant can do – and this what many attorneys do – is forge ahead. One step at a time.

11. AGEIST REMARKS

Ageist remarks are the most commonplace evidence of age discrimination. A manager leaves little to the imagination when s/he says, "We're only sending young people to the training." Ageist comments should be powerful evidence of an employer's discriminatory intent.

The EEOC filed a lawsuit in 2010 against Hawaii Healthcare Professionals, Inc. after the owner told a manager to fire a 54-year-old office coordinator because she "looks old, sounds old on the telephone" and is "like a bag of bones." [1] The case was settled two years later for $193,236.

Courts today are more sensitive about the impact of ageist remarks than they were in the past but many still do not view ageist comments with the same gravity as racist or sexist speech.

Ageist comments, without more, may not be enough.

Discriminatory comments in general may be considered inconsequential "stray remarks" if a significant period of time

---

[1] *EEOC v. Hawaii Healthcare Professionals, Inc. a/k/a Hawaii Professional HomeCare Services, Inc.*, Case No. CV-10-00549 BMK (2010).

elapses between the remark(s) and the alleged discriminatory act or in cases where the supervisor who uttered the remark did not play a deciding role in the decision-making process that led to the alleged discriminatory act.[2]

One federal appeals court refused to permit a plaintiff to even introduce ageist remarks as evidence in a case involving an allegedly discriminatory reduction in force. The court said the remarks were unduly prejudicial to the employer![3] In that case, a supervisor said that "young people [are] taking over up front." Another supervisor protested when an employee called them both "old timers." He retorted:"[D]on't categorize me in that with you." It would seem the remarks revealed sensitivity toward aging and older workers. Yet the appeals court said the comments were too abstract, irrelevant and unduly prejudicial to the employer.

There may be a tipping point with respect to ageist comments in the workplace. Courts seem to be more sympathetic when older worker are subject to "repeated profane references ... on almost a daily basis within the work setting..."[4]

A Texas company, Central Freight Lines, agreed in 2010 to pay $400,000 to settle a lawsuit brought by the EEOC that

---

[2] *Jackson v. Cal-Western Packaging Corp.*, 602 F. 3d 374 (5th Circuit 2010).

[3] *Chappel v. GTE Products Corp.*, 803 F.2d 261, 268 n.2 (6th Cir. 1986).

[4] *Dediol v. Best Chevrolet, Inc.*, 655. F.3d 435, 439 (5th Cir. 2011).

alleged the company conducted a "ruse" reduction in force. The company fired eight dock workers who were over the age of 50, some of whom had worked at the company for more than 20 years, and replaced them with younger workers. The older dock workers were repeatedly called names like "grandpa," "old farts" and "old bastards."[5]

> *Ageist comments often are not deemed as serious as derogatory comments involving race, gender or sexual orientation.*

Conversely, a federal appeals court Missouri issued a 9 – to–3 ruling in 2014 to dismiss an age discrimination case filed by a 76-year-old security guard who was fired after his supervisor repeatedly told him he was "too old" to be working and that he should "hang up [his] Superman cape and retire."[6] The court said the ageist remarks were not sufficient to show the guard's termination was based on age, noting the supervisor who uttered the remarks was only one of three officials who made the decision to fire the security guard. The court also said the security guard failed to show the company's explanation for his termination offered was mere pretext. The company contended the guard was fired because he left his shift an hour early.

---

[5] *Ricky L. Curry et al. v. Central Freight Lines Inc.*, No. 3:10-cv-01954, (U.S.D.C. Northern District of Texas, 2010).
[6] *Johnson v. Securitas Sec. Services, USA, Inc.*, 769 F.3d 605 (8th Cir. 2014).

The irony of the Missouri court's "Superman" decision is apparent when it is contrasted with a case involving an offensive comment based on race. In 2013, a supervisor allegedly made a single offensive racial epithet (she denied it) to an African-American employee. She allegedly shouted "get out of my office n----r." A federal appeals court said "this single incident might well have been sufficient to establish a hostile work environment."[7]

The EEOC issued a landmark decision in 2015 in the case of a gay worker who was denied a promotion after being subjected to homophobic remarks.[8] The complainant said that when he mentioned that he and his partner had attended Mardi Gras in New Orleans his supervisor responded, "We don't need to hear about that gay stuff." He also said his supervisor claimed that he was a "distraction" to others when he discussed his male partner. For the first time in this case, the EEOC said that Title VII of the Civil Rights Act extends to claims of employment discrimination based on sexual orientation.

The point is not that courts should accord less protection to offensive comments that target blacks or gays

---

[7] *Ayissi-Etoh v. Fannie Mae, et al.*, 1.10-cv-01259 (D.C. Cir. April 5, 2013).
[8] in _____ [name of charging party kept secret] v. Foxx, EEOC Appeal No. 2012-24738–FAA-03 (July 15, 2015).

but that ageist comments are equally offensive and just as revealing about the existence of discrimination.

Jurors may be more offended by ageist language than federal judges, who have lifetime appointments and virtual autonomy. A state court jury in New Jersey awarded a high school chemistry teacher $509,000 in damages because she was driven out of her job after changing her mind about retiring at age 60.[9] Jeanne O'Neil told school officials she wanted to keep her job because her husband's health was failing and she needed the medical benefits. Thereafter, her supervisors observed her classroom seven times in four months and told her that her teaching methods were "antiquated," "too traditional," and that she was "regressing" in her ability to teach.[10] The jury decided that O'Neil was the victim of a hostile work environment and constructive discharge. She was awarded $185,000 in back pay, $24,000 in lost benefits and $300,000 for emotional distress.

---

[9] Goldberg, Dan, *Ex-Teacher in Morris County nets more than $500k over age discrimination*, The New Jersey Star-Ledger (Jan. 9, 2012), retrieved on 11/21/15 at http://www.nj.com/news/index.ssf/2012/01/ex-teacher_nets_more_than_500k.html
[10] *O'Neill v. Jefferson Township Bd. of Educ.*,

12. HOSTILE WORK ENVIRONMENT

Harassment is illegal under the ADEA when it creates a hostile work environment. This occurs when a worker aged 40+ is subjected to:

- Unwelcome verbal or physical conduct because the worker is aged 40 or older;

- This harassment creates an environment that a reasonable person would find intimidating, hostile, and offensive;

- The harassment alters a term or condition of the complainant's employment; and/or

- Has the effect of unreasonably interfering with the complainant's work environment.

There is no law in the United State prohibiting workplace bullying. So it is not enough for older workers to show they were harassed in the workplace. To be actionable under the ADEA, workers must show the harassment was motivated by illegal age bias.

Harassment also must rise to a high level of seriousness. The U.S. Supreme Court has emphasized that petty slights, annoyances and isolated incidents (unless extremely serious) do not rise to the level of illegality. A single joke that is in poor taste is likely insufficient to constitute illegal harassment but repeated offensive jokes might rise to the level of being sufficiently serious.

According to the EEOC, harassment includes, but is not limited to, offensive jokes, slurs, epithets or name calling, physical assaults or threats, intimidation, ridicule or mockery, insults or put-downs, offensive objects or pictures, and interference with work performance.[1]

A worker does not have to be the person who was harassed but can be anyone who was affected by the offensive conduct.

The ADEA also prohibits retaliatory harassment against individuals who have opposed age discrimination by, among other things, filing a discrimination charge, testifying, or participating in any way in an investigation, proceeding, or a lawsuit relating to a charge of age discrimination.

Is the Employer Liable?

A key factor in any civil rights case is not necessarily whether a hostile workplace environment exists but whether the employer can be held liable for it. Courts view harassment differently depending upon whether the harasser was a supervisory employee or a co-worker.

---

[1] See EEOC Laws, Regulations, Guidance & MOUs, Harassment, viewed on 12/01/15 at http://www.eeoc.gov/laws/types/harassment.cfm

Supervisor

Employers are automatically liable if the harasser is a supervisor; and

- The hostile work environment led to a tangible job detriment (i.e., termination, demotion, failure to hire, etc.) against the employee; and

- The employer failed to take reasonable steps to prevent and promptly correct the harassing behavior after the victim(s) complained.

Non Supervisor

An employer is liable if the harasser is a non-supervisory employee (i.e., co-worker) or a non-employee over whom the employer had control (i.e., independent contractor, customer) and:

- The employer knew or should have known the worker was being harassed; and

- The employer failed to take immediate and appropriate corrective action.

➤ Who is Considered to be a Supervisor?

Employers are automatically responsible for the unlawful acts of supervisors but who is a supervisor? This answer to this question does not rest upon the job title of the harasser. It involves an analysis of the harasser's job functions. In other words, you may think the harasser is a supervisor because s/he is a team leader but s/he may not be considered a supervisor under the current legal definition of the term.

A supervisor is an individual who:

- Has immediate or higher authority over the employee; and
- Is authorized to undertake or recommend tangible employment decisions affecting an employee.

The U.S. Supreme Court redefined supervisor liability in a controversial 5-to-4 decision in a 2013 race discrimination case, *Vance v. Ball State University.*[2] The *Vance* majority held that an employee is a "supervisor" only if the employer has empowered that employee "to take tangible employment actions against the victim, i.e., to effect a 'significant change in employment status, such as hiring, firing, failing to promote, reassignment with significantly different responsibilities, or a decision causing a significant change in benefits.'"

The majority ruled that Ball State University in Indiana was not liable for the alleged harassment of Maetta Vance, an African-American worker, by university catering specialist Saundra Davis. Vance understood Davis to be her supervisor

---

[2] 133 S. Ct. 2434 (2013).

because Vance directed her work but the majority said Davis was not actually Vance's supervisor because she could not take tangible employment action against Vance.

A real supervisor, according to the Vance majority, has the ability to subject a worker to a tangible employment action that results in a "significant change" in the worker's employment status. A significant change occurs when a worker is hired; fired; not promoted, reassigned with different responsibilities, etc.

Whether an act is tangible depends on the specific circumstances of a case.

A threat is not a tangible employment action if the supervisor does not follow through with the threat.

A threat - such as a threat of termination – may not be considered a tangible employment action unless the supervisor actually brings the power of the enterprise to bear upon the subordinate and the worker suffers direct economic harm. Other actions that may be considered insufficient to be a tangible employment action include a poor performance evaluation, reprimand, placement on paid leave, increased job responsibilities, or revocation of incidental privileges.

No Tangible Employment Action

If a worker is harassed by a supervisor but did not suffer a tangible job detriment, the employer is entitled to mount an affirmative defense to avoid liability. The employer must show that it:

- Exercised reasonable care to prevent and correct the harassment; *and*
- The employee unreasonably failed to take advantage of preventive or corrective opportunities provided by the employer or to otherwise avoid harm.

It is natural for victims of harassment to hope the harassment will stop in time. It may be reasonable if a victim of harassment ignores the first or second incident of harassment. But at some point, a worker's failure to complain about on-the-job harassment may be considered unreasonable.

If the worker fails to complain, employers can argue they had no notice of the hostile workplace environment and, therefore, no opportunity to stop it. But if the worker complains and the employer fails to stop the harassment, the employer will be subject to both laiblity and, potentially, additional damages.

There are circumstances where a failure to complain is reasonable, such as when there is no effective complaint mechanism or the process is unduly difficult, intimidating or ineffective. For example, a complaint process could be deemed to be ineffective if it required a worker to complain to the supervisor who was the harasser. It also could be considered reasonable if a worker did not complain because s/he knew that co-worker(s) had complained but the employer did nothing to stop harassment.

Employer Negligence

In the *Vance* decision, the Supreme Court said that an employer is liable for harassment by non-supervisory employees if the employer was "negligent in failing to prevent harassment from taking place." The Court said the nature and degree of authority wielded by the harasser is an "important factor" in determining employer negligence. Also "relevant," said the Court, is evidence that the employer:

- Failed to monitor the workplace;
- Did not respond to complaints;
- Lacked a system for registering complaints; and,
- Effectively discouraged complaints from being filed.

EEOC: Prevention is the best remedy.

The EEOC notes that prevention is the best tool for addressing workplace harassment. The agency recommends that employers establish an effective complaint or grievance process that lets employees know how and to whom to make a complaint, investigates complaints promptly, and levels appropriate actions against individuals who are found to have engaged in harassment or retaliation.

➢ **Elements of a Hostile Workplace**

To prove a hostile workplace environment, the plaintiff must prove:

1. S/he is aged 40 or above;

2. S/he was subjected to harassment because of age;

3. The nature of the harassment was sufficiently severe or pervasive to alter the conditions of employment and create an abusive or hostile work environment;

4. S/he subjectively perceived the working environment to be abusive or hostile;

5. A reasonable person in the plaintiff's circumstances would objectively view the working environment to be intimidating, hostile or offensive;

6. There is a basis for liability on the part of the employer (i.e., the employer has the minimum number of employees required to sue under the ADEA).

'Objectively' Offensive

A reasonable person in the plaintiff's circumstances must objectively view the working environment to be offensive. The following factors are used to evaluate whether conduct is objectively offensive:

- The pervasiveness or frequency of the discriminatory conduct;

- Its severity;

- Whether it is physically threatening or humiliating, or merely an offensive utterance; and,

- Whether it interferes with an employee's work performance.

How hostile?

Some federal courts have found conditions that many would say border on tortuous to be insufficiently hostile to constitute a hostile workplace, while other courts reflect sensitivity to humiliating ageist taunts and stereotypes.

Courts assess the "totality of the circumstances" to determine if there was a hostile work environment.

A federal appeals court in Louisiana in 2011 recognized a claim of hostile work environment in the case of a 65-year old car salesman, a devout Christian, whose supervisor continually called him derogatory names like "old mother ***," "old man" and "pops."[3] The supervisor also threatened to "kick [his] ass," intimidated him, and provoked fights.

Conversely, a federal court said a 65-year-old teacher in Nashville, TN, was not subjected to a hostile workplace as a result of comments by two assistant principals.[4] One of the

---

[3] *Dediol v. Best Chevrolet, Inc.*, 655 F. 3d (Fifth Cir. 2011).
[4] *Norman v. Metro. Gov't of Nashville & Davidson Cnty.*, No .3:12-cv-1288 (M.D. Tenn. Sept. 30, 2015).

vice-principles said, "[S]ome people don't know when to retire." The other said, "Aren't you ready to retire soon," and "[h]ow old did you say you were?" The teacher characterized the comments as badgering and intimidating. She said she "broke down in tears one time." The court said the comments did not rise to the level of severe and pervasive.

The U.S. Supreme Court has said that for a plaintiff to suffer from a hostile work environment, the workplace must be "permeated with discriminatory intimidation, ridicule, and insult that is sufficiently severe or pervasive to alter the conditions of the victim's employment and [to] create an abusive working environment."[5] Conduct that is "merely offensive" will not suffice to support a hostile work environment action.

Harassment does not have to cause actual psychological harm to constitute a hostile work environment because abusive behavior can detract from an employee's job performance.[6]

Statute of Limitations

A hostile work environment claim can encompass events that occur outside the statute of limitations if at least one incident occurred within the filing period. An older worker can, for example, allege s/he was subject to an extended

---

[5] *Harris v. Forklift Systems, Inc.*, 510 U.S. 17, 21 (1993).
[6] *Harris v. Forklift Systems, Inc.*, 510 U.S. 17 (1993).

campaign of harassment as long as the last incident occurred within the statute of limitations. Some courts say that adverse and discriminatory actions that fall outside the filing period cannot be the basis for damages. They are relevant to show a pattern of abuse and can be considered when determining the extent of over-all liability and damages related to a hostile work environment claim. For example, if a worker was demoted but failed to file a timely EEOC claim, the demotion can still be considered evidence in a hostile workplace claim that falls within the statute of limitations, though the worker cannot recover damages based on the demotion itself.

13. INDIVIDUAL LIABILITY

Suppose a supervisor denies a promotion to a worker because s/he is over the age of 40. Then the supervisor is overheard telling others, "Why doesn't that dinosaur retire?" This conduct is prohibited by the ADEA and the victim may be able to hold the employer liable. But most courts say the ADEA does not permit the victim to sue the individual supervisor.

> *Most courts do not allow a supervisor or coworker to be named as an individual defendant in an ADEA lawsuit.*

The ADEA defines an "employer" as "a person engaged in an industry affecting commerce who has twenty or more employees for each working day in each of twenty or more calendar weeks in the current or preceding calendar year . . . The term also means...any agent of such a person." 29U.S.C. § 630(b).

Most federal circuit courts agree that Congress intended the "any agent" clause to limit, rather than expand, the liability of employers. They take the position that the ADEA does not permit lawsuits against individual defendants.

A contrary opinion was issued by a panel of three judges on the U.S. Court of Appeals for the Sixth Circuit in Ohio in a 2013 sexual harassment case. The panel ruled in *Mengelkamp v. Lake Metropolitan Housing Authority* that an individual qualifies as an "employer" if s/he:

- Serves in a supervisory position,

- Has "significant control over plaintiff's hiring, firing, or conditions of employment," and

- Maintains "the ultimate authority over [the plaintiff's] employment and working conditions.[1]

The decision only applies in the Sixth Circuit, which serves Michigan, Ohio, Kentucky and Tennessee.

Federal law advances through the decisions of the U.S. District Courts of Appeal in the eleven regional circuits and the District of Columbia. If a conflict arises between the federal circuit courts, the U.S. Supreme Court can break the impasse. But the Court has not addressed the issue of whether an individual can be sued under federal civil rights laws.

In *Mengelkamp*, a jury found that the plaintiff's male manager consciously disregarded her rights and engaged in "outrageous" and "flagrant" actions. He was ordered to pay the plaintiff $105,000 in punitive damages. The appeals court panel ruled the manager could be held individually liable because he held a supervisory position, had significant control

---

[1] *Mengelkamp v. Lake Metro. Hous. Authority.*, No. 12-4468 at 22 (6th Cir. Nov. 4, 2013).

over the plaintiff's firing, and was the person in charge of employment conditions.

Congressional Intent?

The majority view is that Congress intended to preclude litigation against individuals to limit the burden of civil rights litigation on small businesses.

The U.S. Court of Appeals for the Seventh Circuit in Chicago, Il, wrote in 1995 that the "limitation" inherent in the "any agent" clause of the Americans with Disabilities Act (ADA) "struck a balance between the goal of stamping out all discrimination and the goal of protecting small entities from the hardship of litigating discrimination claims."[2] The ADA's definition of "employer" mirrors the definitions of "employer" in Title VII and the ADEA.

The Ninth Circuit Court of Appeals in San Francisco, CA, observed in a 1993 decision, "If Congress decided to protect small entities with limited resources from liability [Title VII - employers with less than 15 employees, ADEA - employers with less than 20 employees], it is inconceivable that Congress intended to allow civil liability to run against individual employees."[3]

---

[2] *EEOC v. AIC Security Investigations, Ltd.*, 55 F. 3d 1276 (1995).
[3] *Miller v. Maxwell's International Inc.*, 991 F.2d 583 (9th Cir.1993).

➤ **State Laws**

Individuals may be immune from lawsuits under the ADEA but this is not always the case under state age discrimination laws.

The Missouri Supreme Court ruled *Hill v. Ford, et al.* that the Missouri Human Rights Act contains a broad definition of "employer."[4] The court said the Act is intended to reach not just corporate or public employers but any person acting directly in the interest of the employer, including supervisory employees. Therefore, the court said, supervisors may be individually liable for discriminatory conduct.

The Colorado Discrimination Act (Colo. Rev. Stat. 24-34-402) prohibits discrimination on the basis of disability, race, creed, color, sex, sexual orientation, religion, age, national origin, or ancestry. According to that law: "It shall be a discriminatory or unfair employment practice: For any person, whether or not an employer ... or the employees or members thereof ... to attempt, either directly or indirectly, to commit any act defined in this section to be a discriminatory or unfair employment practice."

Personal Injury Law

There are other potential legal avenues available to sue individuals who participate in severe harassment in the

---

[4] *Hill v. Ford Motor Company, et al.*, 324 F. Supp. 2d 1028 (E.D. Mo. 2004).

workplace. For example, a lawsuit can be based on a state common law tort or personal injury theory, such as negligent infliction of emotional distress, defamation of character, or wrongful discharge. A tort is a cause of action based in the common law that is intended to correct an individual wrong.

14. THE REPLACEMENT WORKER

Age discrimination is not hard to imagine when a 65-year-old worker with excellent evaluations is suddenly replaced by a 30-year -old "go-getter." It is more difficult when the replacement worker is the same age or older than the worker.

> *Savvy employers intent upon discriminating may replace an older worker with someone close to the worker's age or even older to disguise their intentions.*

An employer may engage in different strategies to avoid the appearance of discrimination. One strategy is to replace an older worker with a worker who is the same age or older. Then, sometime later, the replacement worker retires or is transferred to another position in a company "restructuring." The employer then accomplishes its original goal and appoints the 30-year-old go-getter to the position formerly held by the plaintiff.

The age of the replacement worker, who is also known as the 'comparator,' is important in a disparate treatment case because it can, standing alone, raise an inference of age discrimination.

At one time, a plaintiff could not sue for age discrimination under the ADEA if the replacement worker was age 40 or older. This changed in 1996 when the U.S. Supreme Court ruled the age of the replacement worker is "irrelevant so long as [the plaintiff] has lost out because of age."[1]

But age difference still matters. The Court said "[t]he fact that a replacement is substantially younger than the plaintiff is a far more reliable indicator of age discrimination than is the fact that the plaintiff was replaced by someone outside the protected class." An inference of discrimination cannot be drawn, said the Court, when there is an insignificant difference between the age of the plaintiff and the replacement worker.

> *The Court said the age of the replacement worker can be significant in helping the Court decide whether age discrimination has occurred.*

In recent years, federal appeals courts have tackled the question of how much younger a replacement worker must be to raise a rebuttable inference of age discrimination. A rebuttable presumption is one that the employer must rebut or explain away to dispel. Several courts have concluded that an age difference of less than ten years is not substantial

---

[1] *O'Connor v. Consolidated Coin Caterers*, 517 U.S. 308 (1996).

enough to raise a presumption of age discrimination. These courts hold that a rebuttable presumption of age discrimination only arises when the age difference between a plaintiff and his/her replacement worker is ten years or more.[2]

➢ EEOC says No Bright Line

The U.S. Equal Employment Opportunity Commission takes the position that there is no "bright line" test for when an age difference between an older worker and a replacement worker becomes significant. According to the EEOC, any difference potentially can raise a presumption of age discrimination. The agency issued guidelines to assess the significance of age difference when it is slight:

1. Did the replacement worker previously express an interest in retiring?

2. Does the employer have a history of taking action against older workers that would support an inference of age discrimination?

3. Were age-based comments made in connection with the allegedly discriminatory action?

4. If the slightly younger replacement worker was hired by someone who was outside of the control of the

---

[2] See *France v. Johnson*, No. 13-15534 D.C. No. 4:10-cv-00574- JGZ (August 3, 2015).

person who fired the alleged age discrimination victim, there would be less of an inference of age discrimination since the firing and hiring were separate and independent acts by two different individuals.

The EEOC guidelines reflect an underlying concern that calculating employers would abuse a firm and fast rule that discounts a slight age difference between age discrimination victims and their comparators.

The Burden is on the Complainant

Sandra, 56, a manager at a jewelry store in the Kay Jewelers chain, was demoted after failing to meet her sales quota. She filed an age discrimination lawsuit asserting that the 40-year-old manager of another Kay store also failed to meet the sales quota but was not demoted. She also argued that meeting a sales quota does not adequately reflect how well a manager performs.

Attorneys for Kay Jewelers claimed that Sandra was demoted because she repeatedly failed to reach the store quota, whereas the 40-year-old manager had higher evaluation scores for sales and overall performance.

A federal appeals court ruled that it was not the court's job to decide what type of evaluation system best measures a manager's performance. The court said its job was to decide whether the employer's real reason for demoting Sandra was age discrimination. The court concluded that Sandra failed to prove that Kay Jewelers demoted her "because of" age discrimination.[3]

---

[3] *Simpson v. Kay Jewelers*, 142 F.3d 639 (3rd Cir. 1998).

15. DISPARATE IMPACT: POLICIES & PRACTICES

"Age has no reality except in the physical world."
— Gabriel García Márquez

A lesser used theory of age discrimination is the "disparate impact" theory, which is invoked when an employer's policy or practice appear to be neutral but harms older workers more than younger workers.[1] Disparate impact claims often involve tests and procedures used by employers to screen job applicants or to select workers to be laid off in a reduction-in-force.

Unlike intentional discrimination, the disparate impact theory does not require a plaintiff to prove intent to discriminate. This theory is about the "consequences" of an employer's actions, rather than the employer's "mindset."[2]

The focus of the disparate impact theory is the consequence of a discriminatory practice or policy, not the employer's intent.

The disparate impact theory under the ADEA permits more discrimination than is permissible under Title VII of the

---

[1] 29 U.S.C. § 623 (F)(1).
[2] *Texas Dept. of Housing and Community Affairs et al. v. Inclusive Communities Project, Inc., et al.* 576 U.S. __ , 2 (June 25, 2015).

Civil Rights Act, which prohibits discrimination based on race, sex, color, religion and national origin.[3] The ADEA permits discrimination that is based on "reasonable factors other than age."[4] Title VII requires employers to show that discrimination was the result of "business necessity" and that the practice or policy had the least possible discriminatory impact.

Courts generally have made it difficult to prove disparate impact discrimination. The U.S. Supreme Court in a 2015 case involving discrimination in housing signaled its reluctance to interfere in matters of business that affect the state of the economy.[5] The Court said disparate impact liability "must be limited so employers ... are able to make the practical business choices and profit-related decisions that sustain the free-enterprise system." Moreover, the Court said, "Policies, whether governmental or private, are not contrary to the disparate-impact requirement unless they are 'artificial, arbitrary, and unnecessary barriers.'"

➤ Elements of Disparate Impact

Here are the basic elements that plaintiffs must show to establish a *prima facie* case of disparate impact discrimination:

---

[3] *Smith v. City of Jackson*, 544 U.S. 228, 240 (2005).
[4] *Smith*, 544 U.S. at 233 (quoting the ADEA)
[5] *Texas Dept. of Housing and Community Affairs et al. v. Inclusive Communities Project, Inc., et al.* 576 U.S. __ (June 25, 2015).

1. The worker was 40 years of age or older at the time of the employer's adverse employment action (i.e., discharge, failure to hire or demotion). *See* 29 U.S.C. § 631 (a).

2. The employer used a specific test, requirement, practice, or selection criteria that had an adverse or disproportionate impact on employees or job applicants who were 40 years of age or older.[6]

3. The plaintiff suffered an adverse employment action because of that test, requirement, practice, or selection criteria. [7]

"Specific" Practice

The U.S. Supreme Court in 2005 ruled that plaintiffs must identify the specific policy or practice that caused the discrimination.[8] "It is not enough to simply allege that there is a disparate impact on workers, or point to a generalized policy that leads to such an impact. The employee is responsible identifying the specific employment practice responsible for any observed statistical disparities."[9]

Workers must identify the specific practice, policy or action that caused the age discrimination.

---

[6] *Smith v. City of Jackson*, 544 U.S. 228, 232 (2005).
[7] *Pottenger v. Potlatch Corp.*, 329 F.3d 740, 750 (9th Cir.2003).
[8] *Smith v. City of Jackson*, 544 U.S. 228, 232 (2005).
[9] *Smith v. Jackson*, 544 U.S. 228 (2005).

Even the Court acknowledged that it is not a "trivial burden" for plaintiffs to identify the specific practice that caused the discriminatory impact [10] The employer, after-all, was responsible for the alleged discrimination. Plaintiffs are not entitled to demand employee records and documents through court-ordered discovery until they establish a prima facie case of age discrimination. But the case may be dismissed before such discovery is possible if the plaintiff cannot identify the specific practice that caused the discrimination.

Not surprisingly, one study found that federal judges dismiss 77 percent of all employment discrimination cases prior to discovery when the employer files a motion for summary judgment.[11] The rate of dismissal is much higher for discrimination claims than for other business litigation. For example, the dismissal rate for contract cases (which normally involve two businesses) was only 53 percent.

---

[10] *Smith v. Jackson*, 544 U.S. 228 (2005).

[11] See Kevin M. Clermont & Stewart J. Schwab, *Employment Discrimination Plaintiffs in Federal Court: From Bad to Worse?* 3 Harv. L. & Pol'y Rev. 103, 109 (2009) ("[R]esults in the federal courts disfavor employment discrimination plaintiffs, who are now foreswearing use of those courts." id. at 104.); *See also*, Hon. Denny Chin, *Summary Judgment in Employment Discrimination Cases: A Judge's Perspective*, 57 N.Y.L. Schl. L. Rev. 671 at 673 (2012-2013).

➢ Reasonable Factor Other Than Age

The Reasonable Factor Other Than Age (RFOA) defense is the standard employer defense in disparate impact cases. Once the plaintiff identifies a specific business policy, practice or action that caused the discriminatory impact, the employer argues that "the differentiation is based on reasonable factors other than age."[12] A police department asserts, for example, that applicants were required to pass a rigorous physical fitness test to insure they are capable of pursuing and apprehending suspects.

Reasonable Factor Other Than Age Defense

The employer must show:

1. A factor other than age;
2. A legitimate business purpose; and
3. A reasonable relationship between the two.

* The employer is not required under the ADEA to tailor the factor narrowly to minimize its disparate impact on older workers.

The U.S. Supreme Court ruled in a 1981 sex discrimination case that a "satisfactory explanation" by the employer "destroys the legally mandatory inference of discrimination arising from the plaintiff's initial evidence."[13]

---

[12] 29 U.S.C. §623 (F)(1).
[13] *Texas v. Burdine*, 450 U.S. 248, Note 1 (`1981).

The burden is thus on the plaintiff to show that the employer's RFOA defense was not reasonable.

There is no easily applicable definition for what is reasonable. The answer depends upon the specific facts and circumstances of the case. Ultimately, it may boil down to a judgment call by the court.

What is Reasonable?

The city of Jackson, Miss., awarded higher raises to police with five or fewer years of tenure than to officers with five or more years of tenure. Clearly, the city's policy had a disparate impact on older workers.

However, the U.S. Supreme Court ruled 5-to-3 in the 2005 case of *Smith v. Jackson* that the plan was a "reasonable" method of raising police salaries to match those in surrounding communities.[14]

Would the Court have ruled the same way if Jackson's plan was to distribute raises based upon race, gender or religious affiliation? That is almost inconceivable. The case shows that discrimination which would be illegal under Title VII of the Civil Rights Act is legal under the ADEA. The case also

---

[14] 544 U.S. 228 (2005).

raises the question of why the nation's highest court picks winners and losers in employment discrimination cases.

◆

The EEOC and the RFOA Defense

Predicting what a court considers to be "reasonable" discrimination is no easy task. But it is apparent that the U.S. Supreme Court's view reasonableness is narrower than that of the EEOC.

The EEOC in 2012 issued regulations interpreting the RFOA defense in ADEA cases. The EEOC defines a reasonable factor other than age as one that is "objectively reasonable when viewed from the position of a prudent employer mindful of its responsibilities under the ADEA under the circumstances."[15] The "prudent employer" concept is derived from personal injury law and assumes that an employer has a duty to be aware of the consequences of its choices.

To establish an RFOA defense under the ADEA, the EEOC states than an employer must show the challenged employment practice was:

- Reasonably designed to further or achieve a *legitimate* business purpose; and,

---

[15] 29 U.S.C. § 1625.7 (e)(1).

- Administered in a way that reasonably achieves that purpose in light of the particular facts and circumstances that were known, or should have been known, to the employer.

The EEOC says an RFOA must be "reasonably designed and administered to achieve a legitimate business purpose in light of the circumstances, including its potential harm to older workers."

The EEOC issued a series of "relevant considerations" designed to help employers navigate the RFOA defense. The EEOC suggests that employers consider:

- The extent to which a factor is related to the employer's stated business purpose;
- The extent to which the employer defined the factor accurately and applied the factor fairly and accurately, including whether managers and supervisors were given guidance or training about how to apply the factor in such a way as to avoid discrimination;
- The extent to which the employer limited supervisors' discretion to assess employees subjectively, particularly when the criteria that the supervisors use are subject to negative age-based stereotypes;

- The extent to which the employer assessed the adverse impact of its employment practice on older workers; and,

- The degree of harm to individuals within the protected age group, including the extent of injury and the numbers of persons adversely affected, and the extent to which the employer took steps to reduce the harm in light of the burden of undertaking such steps.

The EEOC says that all of these factors are not required to establish the RFOA defense. Indeed, the Agency states there could be a situation where an RFOA defense is upheld absent any of the above considerations.

Layoffs to Achieve Cost Savings

The U.S. Supreme Court established "cost savings" as a valid defense to age discrimination in a 1993 case where a worker was fired a few weeks prior to becoming eligible for vesting in his company's pension plan. [16] The Court said the two concepts- age discrimination and cost savings- are analytically distinct. It ruled the employer in the 1993 case was

---

[16] *Hazen Paper Co. v. Biggins*, 507 U.S. 604 (1993).

not necessarily motivated by age discrimination when it fired the worker.

However, some courts have ruled that employers do not have unlimited discretion to fire older workers to achieve cost savings.

Associated Underwriters, Inc. was sued for age discrimination after it terminated seven employees in a reduction-in-force in 2008. The company claimed the terminations were necessary because of financial difficulties. Then, a company official sent an email to the firm's health insurance provider seeking a rate decrease on the grounds the company had fired its "oldest and sickest employees."

One of those fired was Marjorie Tramp, who was over the age of 65 and had refused to use Medicare instead of the company's health care plan. She was fired for "poor performance."

A federal appeals court in 2014 refused to dismiss an age discrimination lawsuit filed by Tramp.[17] The court said the relationship between age and health care costs is not *as* analytically distinct as that of age and pension eligibility. "Certain considerations, such as health care costs, could be a proxy for age in the sense that if the employer supposes a correlation

---

[17] *Tramp v. Associated Underwriters, Inc.,* 768 F.3d 793 (8th Cir. 2014).

between the two factors and acts accordingly, it engages in age discrimination," the court ruled.

The appeals court said a reasonable jury could find that the company fired Tramp because it believed (incorrectly, as it turned out) that health care rates increase with an employee's age.

Even if employers do genuinely seek cost savings, the EEOC expects them to minimize the risk of age discrimination by providing managers with guidance about how to identify the least productive employees using objective, rather than subjective, criteria.

DISPARATE IMPACT

- Employer adopts a facially neutral policy or rule that has a different and adverse effect on workers aged 40+.
- There is no requirement to prove intent: the focus is on the impact of the policy/rule rather than the employer's mindset.

Defense

- Reasonable Factor Other than Age (RFOA).
- Factor must relate to a legitimate business purpose.

Statistical Evidence

Many courts expect plaintiffs who file a disparate impact case to offer statistical evidence "of a kind and degree sufficient to show that the practice or policy in question has caused the exclusion of applicants because of their membership in a protected group."[18] This evidence does not have to prove causation to a degree of scientific certainty but should be significant enough to reveal a disparity that cannot be accounted for by chance. In other words, the statistical evidence does not have to demonstrate a 100 percent probability of discrimination but must be significant enough to raise an inference of discrimination.[19]

The EEOC's Uniform Guidelines on Employee Selection Criteria addresses employee selection procedures (i.e. hiring, retention, dismissal) under Title VII of the Civil Rights Act. These guidelines hold that a selection rate for any race, sex, or ethnic group that is less than four-fifths (4/5ths) or eighty percent (80%) of the selection rate for the group with the highest selection rate is considered to be a substantially different rate of selection. A question would be raised, for example, if 50 percent of white applicants receive a passing score on a test, but only 10 percent of the African-

---

[18] *Watson v. Fort Worth Bank*, 488 U.S. 977(1988)

[19] *EEOC v. Joint Apprenticeship Committee of Joint Industry Bd. of Elec. Industry*, 186 F.3d 110, 117 (2d Cir. 1999).

Americans who took the test passed.[20] The guidelines have been criticized by some courts.

Expectations with respect to age discrimination generally are much lower than for discrimination on the basis of race or sex. If a test or other selection procedure has a disparate impact based on age, the employer is only required to show that the test or device chosen was a *reasonable* one.

Statistical evidence also may be useful in a disparate treatment case alleging *intentional* age discrimination.

---

[20] 29 C.F.R. Â§ 1607.4 (D) and 1607.16 29 C.F.R. Â§ 1607.4 (D) and 1607.16 R.

16. BENEFIT PLANS

Congress amended the ADEA in 1990 after the U.S. Supreme Court ruled that employee benefit plans were not covered by the ADEA. Congress passed the Older Workers Benefit Protection Act ("OWBPA") to prohibit discrimination against older workers "in all employee benefits except when age-based reductions in employee benefit plans are justified by significant cost considerations."[1]

To receive equal benefits, all workers must be provided the same payment options, the same type of benefits and the same amount of benefits. However, the OWBPA permits employers to provide lower benefits to older workers in limited circumstances, such as where the cost of such benefits increases with an employee's age.[2]

If an employer provides a lower benefit to older workers, it must justify the lower benefit. Typically, employers use one of two defenses:

1. The employer shows that it spends as much, or incurs equal cost, for the lesser benefits that it provided to

---

[1] Pub. L. No. 101-433, 104 Stat. 978 (1990).
[2] 29 U.S.C. § 623(f)(2)(B)(i)

older workers compared to younger workers. This is called the "Equal Cost Defense."

1. The employer shows the total benefit to older workers, after accounting for benefits available from other sources, is no less favorable than the benefit provided to younger workers. This is called the "Offset" Defense.

If the benefits are not the same for older and younger workers, the employer must show that any difference is permitted by law.

Many benefits do not become more expensive to provide as workers get older. For example, an employer cannot use age as a basis to lessen or eliminate paid vacation or sick leave for older workers. And the employer cannot cite cost considerations to justify refusal to hire or the involuntary retirement of older workers.

Employers accused of violating the ADEA cannot plead that age-based benefit disparities meet the requirements of the Employee Retirement Income Security Act of 1974 (ERISA) or the Internal Revenue Code.[3] The EEOC takes the position that ERISA and IRS code do not require an employer to engage in age discrimination.

---

[3] EEOC Compliance Manual, No. 915.003 (Oct. 3, 2000), available at http://www.eeoc.gov/policy/docs/benefits.html#N_8_.

The ADEA permits employers to provide *more* benefits to older workers when there is a reasonable basis to conclude the benefits will counteract problems related to age discrimination. For example, an employer may give a larger severance benefit in a reduction-in-force to a worker who is 55 years of age than to worker who is only 30 years of age because it is reasonable to anticipate the 55-year-old will have a more difficult time finding new employment.

Employers also can offer older workers additional benefits as part of a valid early retirement incentive plan.

What is equal?

To determine if older workers receive the same benefits, it is necessary to compare similarly situated older and younger workers. The comparators must be similar in ways that are relevant to the benefit, such as having comparable length of service and salary. If there aren't two such workers on the payroll, the comparison is based upon a hypothetical employee who is similarly situated to the older worker in all relevant respects except that s/he is younger.

It does not violate the ADEA for a younger worker with more years of service to receive a proportionately higher benefit than an older employee with fewer years of service. It would violate the ADEA, however, if older workers got a lower benefit than younger workers with the same years of service.

This is a complex topic and these cases tend to be highly fact specific. The limited coverage in this book is intended only to familiarize readers with general considerations.

➤ The Equal Cost Defense

The Equal Cost Defense is applicable only to select benefits that become more costly as employees get older.[4] This includes life insurance, health insurance and disability benefits. Employers can reduce the benefit levels for older workers in these categories but only to the extent necessary to achieve cost equivalency with younger workers. Employers cannot reduce benefits to avoid non-age-based cost increases.

The Equal Cost Defense applies when:

- The benefit in question is more expensive as the age of the employer increases;

- The benefit is part of a *bona fide* employee benefit plan. This plan must accurately describe its terms in writing to all employees and provide benefits in accordance with the terms set forth;

- The plan must explicitly require a lower level or duration of benefits for older workers; and

---

[4] 29 U.S.C. § 623(f)(2)(B)(i).

- The amount of payment made, or cost incurred, on behalf of older workers can be no less than that made, or incurred, on behalf of younger workers.

Balancing Benefits

Acme pays $100 per employee to provide an insurance benefit for each of its employees. Acme's insurer raises the premiums by $150 upon an insured's 62nd birthday, requiring the company to spend more on older workers than younger workers. Acme can reduce the benefit it pays to workers who are aged 62 and older to the extent necessary to reduce its premium cost for each employee to $100.

◆

Employers also can use a benefit "packaging" approach for benefits that become more costly to provide with increasing age. They can decrease one benefit more than would be justified by cost data if they increase another benefit by a corresponding amount. Ultimately, employers must pay the same amount for benefits for all employees regardless of age. The packaged benefit can be no less favorable in the aggregate than it would be if the employer took a benefit-by-benefit approach.

➢ **The Offset Rule**

Benefits that older workers obtain from certain government programs, including Medicare, Social Security and disability benefits, can be used in limited circumstances to offset or reduce employer-provided health and pension costs.

The Offset Rule is applicable only if:

- It is specifically authorized by the ADEA; and,
- Older workers are eligible to receive, from all sources, benefits that are no less favorable than those the employer provides to similarly situated younger employees.

The EEOC used its rule-making authority in 2007 to permit alteration, reduction, or elimination of health benefits for retirees who are eligible for Medicare health benefits.[5] As a result, employers can provide retirees over the age of 65 with reduced health benefits because they are eligible for Medicare. The EEOC rule conflicts with the plain language of the OWBPA but the EEOC argued it was necessary because employers were abandoning retiree health care plans due to fear of being sued for age discrimination. Federal

---

[5] 29 C.F.R. § 1625.32(b).

appeals courts upheld the EEOC's rule as a reasonable, necessary and a proper exercise of the EEOC's authority.[6]

Offset provisions also may apply to long-term disability payments and pension benefit accruals. Complex rules govern all of these exceptions.

Early Retirement Incentives

Employers can offer voluntary early retirement incentive plans (ERIs) to older workers as a financial incentive to encourage them to retire provided the workers receive a larger benefit than they would have otherwise received.

According to the EEOC, an ERI plan can be structured to provide:

- A flat dollar amount.

- Additional benefits based on length of service.

- A percentage of salary.

- Flat dollar or percentage increases in pension benefits.

An employer generally must offer equal ERI benefits to older and younger workers who are similarly situated

An ERI plan is not valid unless it is voluntary and knowing. An employee must be given adequate time and sufficient information to make an informed decision about whether to accept an employer's offer. Specific time limits

---

[6] See e.g. *American Ass'n v. EEOC*, 489 F.3d 558, 565 (3rd Cir. 2007) and *Fulghum v. Embarq Corp.* *in re. Retirees & Emps. of Sprint Corp.), No. 13-3220 (10th Cir. April 27, 2015).

apply. An individual must be given at least 21 days, and a group of employees at least 45 days, to consider a waiver.

- See Chapter 4 on Waiver of ADEA Rights.

17. COLLECTIVE ACTION

"Dare to stand before those you fear and speak your mind, even if your voice shakes."
— *Maggie Kuhn*

The ADEA does not permit class action lawsuits in the same manner as Title VII of the Civil Rights Act, which prohibits discrimination on the basis of race, sex, religion, color and national origin. The ADEA allows a party to request certification to proceed in a "collective action."[1]

The ADEA incorporates a provision from the Fair Labor Standards Act (FLSA) that encourages collective actions on behalf of those who are similarly situated to avoid burdening the court with multiple individual lawsuits.[2]

FLSA protects workers who are cheated out of overtime, holiday pay or the proper wages. Many of FLSA claims involve large groups and small amount of money, which make collective actions more reasonable than individual lawsuits.

Age discrimination is a civil rights violation that is very different than a wage claim and yet both are treated similarly

---

[1] 29 U.S.C. § 216(b).
[2] 29 US.C. 216(b); and see *Hoffmann-La Roche Inc. v. Sperling*, 493 U.S. 165, 170 (1989).

in several respects, including lawsuits that involve multiple plaintiffs.

The U.S. Supreme Court has ruled that trial courts have inherent "managerial responsibility" derived from the FLSA to oversee the joinder of additional parties in an ADEA lawsuit.[3] A collective action, said the Court, "allows age discrimination plaintiffs the advantage of lower individual costs to vindicate rights by the pooling of resources. The judicial system benefits by efficient resolution in one proceeding of common issues of law and fact arising from the same alleged discriminatory activity."[4]

A collective action typically involves a discriminatory practice or action that affects a large group of workers, such as a reduction in force.

The ADEA requires a party to "opt in" to join an age discrimination lawsuit.

A collective action differs from a Title VII class action in several respects. The ADEA requires a party to file a written consent with the court to join or "op in" to a collective action. By contrast, Title VII class action lawsuits require individuals to "opt out" of the lawsuit if they do not want to participate. ADEA plaintiffs generally are not required to meet the strict requirements of a Title VII class action that

[3] *Hoffmann-La Roche*, 493 U.S. at 174.
[4] *Hoffmann-La Roche*, 493 U.S. at 170.

involve a showing of numerosity, typicality, commonality and representativeness of the class.

> *The U.S. Supreme Court said a single collective action is preferable to multiple individual lawsuits relating to the same alleged conduct.*

Under the ADEA, plaintiffs must file a charge that contains allegation(s) of class-wide discrimination to insure the employer has notice of the type of complaint. One court ruled it was insufficient to establish a collective action where a complainant merely stated in the charge that other individuals over the age of 40 had experienced similar discriminatory treatment similar.[5]

The plaintiff must file a motion for certification of the collective action. The court determines if the plaintiff's proposed co-plaintiffs are "similarly situated" to the plaintiff.

A collective action may permit an individual to "piggyback" onto another plaintiff's EEOC charge without having to file their own EEOC charge. However, the original plaintiff's charge must be valid and the piggy backer's claim must arise out of similar discriminatory treatment that occurred within the same time frame.[6]

---

[5] *Rodrigues v. SCM I Invs. LLC*, No. 2:15-cv-128-FtM-29CM 17 (M.D. Fla. Nov. 2, 2015).

[6] See *Calloway v. Partners Nat'l Health Plans*, 986 F.2d 446, 450 (11th Cir. 1993).

➢ **Who is Similarly Situated?**

Most courts undertake a two-step process to determine if prospective plaintiffs are "similarly situated" and thus eligible to join a collective action under the ADEA:

In the first step, the court requires the plaintiff to make a "modest" threshold showing as to whether the plaintiff and proposed members of the collective action are victims of a common policy or plan that violated the law.[7] Plaintiffs must have similar, though not identical, job duties and pay. If satisfied, the court may conditionally certify the class and order the employer to provide a list of names and addresses of potential "opt in" class members.

The court supervises the manner in which potential class members are informed of the existence of the lawsuit and their right to opt in. The parties generally are asked to agree on a written notice and consent form but if an agreement cannot be reached, the court will decide the language of the notice, which usually is mailed to prospective plaintiffs.

Employers typically file a motion to decertify the class at the close of discovery. The court then undertakes a second more stringent factual determination to see if the plaintiffs are in fact "similarly situated."

---

[7] See e.g., *Hoffman v. Sbarro*, 982 F. Supp. 249, 261 (S.D.N.Y. 1997).

In its second review, the court considers the similarity of the employment settings of the individual plaintiffs, various defenses available to the employer with respect to the individual plaintiffs and examines issues of fairness and procedural considerations. If the court decides the plaintiffs are not similarly situated, the court can decertify the class or divide it into subclasses where appropriate.[8]

A Maryland judge in 1995 denied class certification to a worker who was fired by a senior manager because he had simply listed names of other older workers who were fired by the same official. The court said the plaintiff "has not pointed to any company plan or policy to target older employees for termination… the mere listing of names, without more, is insufficient absent a factual showing that the potential plaintiffs are 'similarly situated.'"[9]

In an FLSA case, a court found the plaintiff and potential opt-in plaintiffs to be "similarly situated" based on affidavits and allegations submitted by the plaintiff and admissions by the employer. The evidence, according to the court, was more than sufficient. "Significantly, defendant has twice conceded to the Court that the business practices at

---

[8] See *Cunningham v. Electronic Data Systems Corp.*, 754 F. Supp. 2d 638, 9 (D.F.N.Y. 2010).
[9] *D'Anna v. M/A-COM, Inc., 903 F. Supp. 889 (D. Md. 1995).*

issue in this case are uniform among its stores," the court noted.[10]

---

[10] *Damassia v. Duane Reade, Inc.*, 2009 WL 5841128 (SD New York 2006).

18. RETALIATION

The most common type of complaint received by the EEOC each year involves a charge of retaliation in connection with a discrimination claim. The EEOC logged almost 38,000 charges of retaliation in 2014, which was almost half of the 89,000 charges of all types received by the agency that year.

The ADEA anti-retaliation clause, Section 623 (d), makes it unlawful for an employer to discriminate against an individual because that person has:

- Opposed any practice made unlawful by the ADEA; or,

- Made a charge, testified, assisted, or participated in any manner in an investigation, proceeding, or litigation brought under the ADEA.

The primary purpose of an anti-retaliation provision is to insure that workers are not deterred from exercising their right to complain about illegal discrimination. Without such a clause, the purpose of the ADEA – to stop invidious age discrimination - would be thwarted.

An individual does not have to aged 40 and above to file a retaliation complaint under the ADEA.

"Reasonable" Opposition

All opposition to discrimination is not protected under the ADEA retaliation clause – only opposition that is "reasonable." This is a somewhat vague standard that balances the right of individuals to oppose employment discrimination with an employer's need for a stable and productive work environment.

Opposition to discrimination covers a wide swath of behaviors and activities. For example, the U.S. Supreme Court ruled in a 2009 sexual harassment case that protection from retaliation extends to employees who respond to questions about discrimination in during an internal investigation.[1] "To oppose does not require active or consistent behavior in ordinary discourse," said the Court, "and may be used to speak of someone who has taken no action at all to advance a position beyond disclosing it."

Forms of communication that have been held to be reasonable forms of opposition to discrimination include:

- Making a charge.
- Testifying, assisting or participating in an investigation, proceeding or hearing.
- Writing critical letters to customers.

---

[1] *Crawford v. Metro. Gov't of Nashville & Davidson Cnty.*, 555 U.S. 271, 848 (2009).

- Peaceful picketing and boycotting.[2]
- Staging an informal protest of discriminatory employment practices.
- Making complaints to management in writing.

A federal appeals court in 2006 ruled that opposition to an illegal employment practice must identify the employer and the practice – if not specifically at least by context.[3] That court said the complainant's letter to the company's Human Resources department was too general and vague to constitute reasonable opposition because it did not specifically complain about age discrmination. The letter simply said the complainant felt her position was given to a less qualified person.

Other activities that were not considered to be reasonable opposition include:

- Disruptive and disorderly behavior.
- Unlawful activities, such as threats of violence.
- Photocopying confidential documents related to alleged discrimination and showing them to co-workers.
- Badgering a subordinate employee to provide a witness statement in support of an EEOC charge.

---

[2] *Payne v. McLemore's Wholesale Retail Stores,* 654 F.2d 1130 (5th Cir. 1981).
[3] *Curay-Cramer v. Ursuline Academy, Wilmington,* 450 F.3d 130, 134 (3rd Cir. 2006).

> *An employer cannot fire or refuse to promote an employee because s/he filed a discrimination charge – even if the EEOC later determines no discrimination occurred.*

➢ Adverse Action

The ADEA's retaliation provision comes into play when an individual who has opposed age discrimination is subject to an "adverse action" by an employer. Examples of adverse actions are:

- Termination.

- Refusal to hire.

- Denial of promotion.

- Threats.

- Unjustified negative evaluations.

- Withholding a letter of recommendation.

- Unjustified negative references.

- Increased surveillance.

- Any other actions, such as an assault or unfounded civil or criminal charges, that are likely to deter reasonable people from pursuing their rights.

Courts have ruled that adverse actions do not include petty slights and annoyances, such as a stray negative comment, snub, or a negative comment that is justified by an employee's poor work performance or history.

A federal appeals court upheld a claim of retaliation in 1991 against the American Chemical Society (ACS), which cancelled a public event to honor a 70-year-old chemist after learning that he filed an EEOC charge complaining that ACS forced him to retire. The court said "ACS's action in aborting a 'rare and prestigious,' and highly public, honor for an employee on the eve of its occurrence simply cannot be dismissed... as the inconsequential withdrawal of a mere 'gratuity.'"[4]

It would not be an adverse action if a worker who filed an ADEA complaint was terminated because of verifiable misconduct, such as excessive absenteeism or neglect of job duties because retaliation would not be the *reason* for the adverse action.

In another case, an appeals court in 2015 rejected a retaliation claim in a case in which an older worker was fired after complaining to management that his supervisor told him there were too many "old farts" on the payroll. The court said eight to ten months had elapsed between the comment and the worker's dismissal and said the worker could not establish a "causal link" between the two occurrances.[5]

---

[4] *Passer v. American Chemical Soc.*, 935 UF.2d 322 (D.C. Cir. 1991).
[5] *Goudeau v. National Oilwell Varco, LP*, No. 14-20241 (5th Cir. July 16, 2015).

An appeals court in Ohio ruled in 2014 that the involuntary lateral transfer of Robert Deleon, 53, a Hispanic maintenance supervisor, to a position for which he had applied nine months earlier constituted an adverse employment action. The court reasoned the working conditions of the new position – loud noise and diesel fumes - were sufficiently objectively intolerable to a reasonable person.[6]

When Deleon initially applied for the job, another applicant was selected. Deleon was involuntarily transferred to the post after the successful applicant left and an external candidate declined the job. When he initially applied, prior to his involuntary transfer, Deleon had asked for a "hazard pay" raise and an additional employee. These were not forthcoming. Deleon was terminated after he received a poor evaluation and a stress-related mental breakdown.

---

[6] *Deleon v. Kalamazoo County Road Commission.* 739 F.3d 914 (6th Cir. 2014).

A Bad Reference

John, 43, left his job a few months after filing an age discrimination complaint with the EEOC. He then learned the company was making negative comments about his job performance to prospective employers. John knew that his former employer had a strict policy of refusing to provide information about ex-employees to outsiders. The departure from its own policy is evidence the company had engaged in illegal retaliation against John for having filed an age discrimination complaint.

♦

Harder to Prove

The U.S. Supreme Court made it more difficult to prove retaliation in 2013 when it established a new standard of causation in retaliation cases. Formerly, a plaintiff had only to show that retaliation was one of the motives for the adverse employment action suffered by the complainant. Now plaintiffs must show the employer would not have taken the complained of adverse action "but for" the claimant's protected activity. In other words, the complainant must show that retaliation was the determinative reason for the adverse employment action and not just a factor.

In *University of Texas Southwestern Medical Center v. Nassar,* the Court ruled that a retaliation claimant "must establish that his or her protected activity was a but-for cause of the alleged adverse action by the employer."[7] In that case, Dr. Naiel Nassar, a former faculty member of the University of Texas Southwestern Medical Center (UTSW), alleged that UTSW denied him a job in retaliation for a prior resignation letter that alleged race discrimination at the center. Nassar's resignation letter accused his supervisor of making derogatory comments about Nassar's Middle Eastern heritage. A jury had awarded Nassar $438,167.66 in back pay and $3,187,500 in compensatory damages. That award was overturned when the Court ruled 5-to-4 that the judge failed to instruct the jury on the proper standard of causation.

Independent Claim

A retaliation claim can be upheld even if the underlying charge of age discrimination is found to have no merit. Individuals are protected against retaliation for opposing perceived discrimination if they had a reasonable and good faith belief that the opposed practices were unlawful. This

---

[7] *University of Texas Southwestern Medical Center v. Nassar,* 133 S. Ct. 2517 (2013).

means that an employer that is cleared of a charge of age discrimination still faces significant damages for retaliating against the alleged victim and/or others in connection with the underlying discrimination charge.

The Dreaded Weekend Shift

Ted complained to his office manager that his supervisor promoted a younger worker with less experience. His complaint represented protected opposition to age discrimination because he had a reasonable and good faith belief that the promotion was discriminatory.

Ted's supervisor resented his complaint and scheduled him to work four consecutive weekend shifts. The shift formerly was rotated among four staff members, so each worked the weekend shift once in a month. Ted complained that the scheduling was retaliatory to no avail.

Ted was not a victim of age discrimination because the younger worker had a relevant qualification that Ted lacked. However, Ted was a victim of illegal retaliation by his employer - his supervisor's punitive assignment of Ted to the dreaded weekend shift.

♦

➤ Elements of Retaliation

The steps required to prove retaliation are the same basic steps that a plaintiff must take to demonstrate disparate treatment or intentional discrimination. *See* Chapter 10, Disparate Treatment (Intentional Discrimination)

A plaintiff can demonstrate retaliation by providing direct evidence - such as a statement by a supervisor the employer's actions were taken in response to her protected activity. Plaintiffs who have only circumstantial evidence must use the McDonnell Douglas burden shifting framework to establish a *prima facie* case of retaliation.

Under the McDonnell Douglas burden shifting framework, plaintiffs must show that they:

- Engaged in protected activity,
- The employer knew of their exercise of their protected civil right,
- The employer thereafter took an employment action adverse to the plaintiff, and

- There was a causal connection between the protected activity and the adverse employment action.[8]

If the complainant successfully establishes a *prima facie* case, the burden shifts to the employer to articulate a legitimate, nondiscriminatory reason for its actions. The complainant must then show by a preponderance of the evidence that the supposedly legitimate reason offered by the employer is not the real reason but is a pretext intended to hide illegal retaliation.

---

[8] *See EEOC v. Avery Dennison Corp.*,104 F.3d 858, 860(6th Cir. 1997).

19. DAMAGES

The Age Discrimination in Employment Act has a split personality. The substantive provisions of the ADEA are patterned after Title VII of the Civil Rights Act but the damages portion is patterned after the Fair Labor Standards Act of 1938 (FLSA). Title VII is a civil rights law while the FLSA governs the payment of the minimum wage and overtime. Thus, age discrimination is essentially treated like a failure to pay overtime.

The difference between Title VII and the ADEA does not reflect upon the harm of age discrimination as compared to other types of discrimination. It boils down to a procedural matter.

The U.S. Congress in 1964 voted down a measure to include age as a protected class in Title VII, which prohibits discrimination on the basis of race, sex, color, national origin and religion. Congress decided further study was needed on the subject of age discrimination.

Three years later, when Congress passed the ADEA, the EEOC was swamped with Title VII complaints. Congress assigned responsibility for the ADEA to the U.S. Department of Labor (DOL). To make it easier for the DOL to enforce the ADEA, Congress patterned the ADEA's damages provisions after the other major law that was enforced by the DOL, the FLSA.

Congress in 1978 switched responsibility for the ADEA from the DOL to the EEOC but did not feel it was necessary to revise the ADEA's damages provisions to mirror that of Title VII.

The bottom line is that ADEA plaintiffs are shortchanged when it comes to damages. Because the FLSA is concerned only with failure to pay proper wages, a plaintiff who prevails in an ADEA case is reimbursed only for monetary loss. [1] If there is no monetary loss, a victorious plaintiff gets nothing at all.

An ADEA plaintiff is entitled to recover only for monetary loss.

The ADEA, unlike Title VII, does not allow a plaintiff to recover compensatory damages (i.e. emotional distress) or punitive damages. In lieu of punitive damages, the ADEA, like the FLSA, provides a remedy of liquidated damages - which is double the award of back pay – if the plaintiff can prove "willful" age discrimination.

The ADEA damages formula limits the deterrent effect of the ADEA by limiting the risk faced by employers.

---

[1] See *Lorillard v. Pons*, 434 U.S. 575, 582 (1978)

Employers that engage in age discrimination are no less guilty than employers who engage in discrimination on the basis of race, sex, color, national origin or religion. Yet, ADEA complainants are not entitled punitive damages.

Moreover, age discrimination victims are denied just compensation. The ADEA minimizes their suffering by denying them compensation for emotional distress. Yet, victims of age discrimination suffer the same anger, humiliation, anxiety, rage, bitterness, and frustration as other discrimination victims.

There is no justification for treating age discrimination differently but, for 50 years, this has been the law of the United States.

No punitive damages or damages for emotional distress under the ADEA.

The schizophrenic nature of the ADEA is one reason that so many attorneys bundle ADEA claims with other claims, such as discrimination on the basis of race, sex or disability, wrongful termination and retaliation.

➤ Injunctive Relief

In other contexts, damages are intended to restore plaintiffs to the position that they would have occupied had the discrimination had not occurred. The focus of the ADEA, however, is to reimburse plaintiffs for any monetary loss suffered. The ADEA does, however, direct courts to "grant such legal or equitable relief as may be appropriate to effectuate the purposes" of the Act.[2] This is a forward-looking remedy that is intended to prevent further damage to plaintiff(s).

Injunctive relief can take many forms. A court may order an employer to permanently refrain from engaging in age discrimination or retaliation. For example, the EEOC in 2004 obtained a permanent injunction to prevent an employer from requiring employees who were being terminated in a reduction in force to waive their rights to file a discrimination charge with the EEOC in exchange for receiving a severance payment.[3] The EEOC argued the waiver constituted per se retaliation in violation of the ADEA.

Injunctive relief is intended to prevent future harm.

Courts possess "broad discretion . . . in fashioning relief.[4] Moreover, a district court's award of equitable and injunctive relief is subject to reversal only for abuse of discretion or a clear error of law.

---

[2] 29 U.S.C. § 626(b).
[3] *Equal Employment Opportunity Comm. v. SunDance Rehab. Corp.*, 328 F.Supp.2d 826, 828 (N.D. Ohio 2004).
[4] *Malarkey v. Texaco, Inc.*, 938 F.2d 1204, 1215 (1993).

➢ **Back Pay**

Most age discrimination cases involve job loss so back pay is often an important consideration. Back pay is the value of the salary and benefits that a worker would have received if s/he had not terminated. Back pay is awarded from the time of the discriminatory act or occurrence until the harm suffered by the plaintiff is redressed.

Plaintiffs must demonstrate with reasonable certainty the amount of economic harm they suffered as a result of the alleged discrimination. Back pay must be based on reasonable expectations and not sheer speculation.[5]

Back pay can include:

- Wages and salary.

- Health Insurance.

- Overtime.

- Shift differentials.

- Commissions.

- Tips.

- Cost of living increases.

- Merit increase.

- Raises due to promotion.

---

[5] See *Zhang v. Am. Gem Seafoods, Inc.*, 339 F.3d 1020, 1040 (9th Cir. 2003) (history of bonuses justified award); *Neufeld v. Searle Lab.*, 884 F.2d 335, 342 (8th Cir. 1991) (denying recovery of future bonuses as speculative).

- Fringe benefits, including annual sick leave, vacation pay, pension and retirement benefits, stock options and bonus plans, savings plan contributions, cafeteria plan benefits, profit-sharing benefits and medical and life insurance benefits.

- Compensation for increased tax liability when back pay is awarded in one lump sum.

- Interest on back pay awards.[6]

The amount of back pay awarded can be diminished by the compensation and benefits received by the worker from other sources during the computation period. This would include earnings from a subsequent job. Welfare or unemployment compensation benefits are not considered earnings.

Public assistance and unemployment compensation do not reduce an award of back pay.

Limits on Back Pay

Employers often seek to limit a back pay award by arguing that the complainant failed to act to mitigate the damages stemming from the discriminatory action.

Plaintiffs who lose their jobs are expected to use "due diligence" to look for "substantially equivalent" work, even if

---

[6] Civil Rights Act of 1991, Section 114, codified at 42 USC 2000e-16(d).

it doesn't pay as much.[7] A plaintiff doesn't have to accept inferior employment but cannot insist upon an identical job with the same wages. If a plaintiff finds a job that pays less, the plaintiff is entitled to the difference in wages between the old job and the new job. Plaintiffs may be required to provide evidence documenting the efforts they took to secure alternative employment.

Other theories used by employers to shorten the back-pay accrual period include:

- ✓ The plaintiff refused an unconditional offer of reinstatement.
- ✓ The plaintiff was unable to work because s/he was in poor health.
- ✓ The plaintiff committed misconduct or fraud (i.e. lied on his or her resume).
- ✓ The amount should reflect that most employees in the plaintiff's position do not remain with the same employer for long periods of time.

In a 2005 case, the EEOC found that a postal worker who prevailed on an ADEA claim was properly denied back pay because she signed a statement to the effect that she did not seek outside employment during the back pay period.[8]

---

[7] *Ford Motor Co. v. EEOC*, 458 U.S. 219, 231 (1982).
[8] *Johnson v. United States Postal Service*, EEOC Appeal No. 01A51490 (September 29, 2005).

Plaintiffs can argue their efforts to find new employment were rendered futile because they were terminated by the employer for cause or their efforts were impaired because they suffered significant psychological or physically injuries as a result of the employer's misconduct.

➤ Reinstatement

Reinstatement is said to be the preferred remedy for age discrimination because it makes employees "whole" by returning them to the same economic position they occupied before being wrongfully discharged.

The employer's liability for back pay ends if it extends an offer of reinstatement to the plaintiff for a position that is "substantially equivalent" to the one that was lost or sought. The position should be close in its responsibilities and compensation to the plaintiff's former position. However, a plaintiff should not be expected to report to a supervisor who was involved in the complained of discrimination or harassment.

> *Reinstatement is the preferred remedy for age discrimination but it is not always possible.*

If a plaintiff's former position was filled by another employee who was innocent of the discrimination, the plaintiff must wait for the next job. Relief for victims does not include "bumping employees previously occupying jobs."[9] A plaintiff who is to be reinstated is entitled to be paid until an appropriate job becomes available.

Sometimes there is such hostility between the parties that reinstatement is not practical. A federal judge found the requisite animosity between a former corporate counsel and his employer, Union Carbide Corporation.[10] The judge said Union Carbide had exhibited "such hostility and outrage" against the plaintiff that he would be "ostracized and excluded from the functions of giving counsel." The judge said the hostility between the parties was so intense that reinstatement was impossible.

When reinstatement is not possible, practical or appropriate, the plaintiff is entitled to "front pay" at the court's discretion.

➢ Front Pay

Front pay is a reasonable monetary award of future lost earnings, including salary and benefits. Front pay also may compensate the plaintiff for any difference in pay earned in a new job as compared to the old job.

The U.S. Supreme Court has said that front pay is an equitable remedy that may be awarded for lost compensation

---

[9] *Fire Fighters Local 1784 v. Stotts*, 467 U.S. 561, 579 n.11 (1984).
[10] *Whittlesley v. Union Carbide*, 742 F.2d 724 (2d Cir. 1984).

"between judgment and reinstatement or in lieu of reinstatement."[11]

Front pay is an equitable remedy to compensate a plaintiff for future losses.

Front pay is appropriate when:

- A subsequent working relationship between the parties would be hostile.

- No positions are currently available in the company.

- The company has ceased operations.

- The employer has a record of long-term resistance to anti-discrimination efforts.

- The plaintiff is approaching retirement and the front-pay period is of short duration.

The plaintiff must provide the court with essential data to calculate a reasonable front pay award. Courts tend to exclude speculative losses, such as potential matching contributions to a 401(k) plan.[12]

To determine the amount of front pay, courts may consider the age of the plaintiff; the amount of time that was reasonable for the plaintiff to obtain a comparable position; how long the plaintiff worked for the employer or previous

---

[11] *Pollard v. E.I. du Pont de Nemours & Co.*, 532 U.S. 843, 852 (2001).
[12] *See Buonanno v. AT&T Broadband, LLC*, 313 F. Supp. 2d 1069, 1085-86 (D. Colo. 2004).

employers; and how long employees in a similar positions had worked for the employer.

➤ Liquidated Damages

Liquidated damages are available under the ADEA if the plaintiff can show the employer's violation was "willful."[13] The amount of liquidated damages is generally double the amount of the back pay award. Some courts hold that liquidated damages are a form of compensation and are not meant to penalize or punish the employer.[14]

The U.S. Supreme Court ruled in 1985 that a violation of the ADEA is willful when an employer "knew or showed reckless disregard" for whether its conduct was prohibited by the ADEA.[15] The Court said an ADEA violation is not willful if the employer acted "reasonably and in good faith in attempting to determine whether a particular action would violate the ADEA"[16] In the case of *Trans World Airlines v. Thurston*, the airline consulted with its counsel and negotiated with the union to modify its collective bargaining agreement in an effort to conform to the ADEA.[17]

---

[13] 29 U.S.C. § 626(b).
[14] *Elwell v. Univ. Hosp. Home Care Serv.*,276 F.3d 832, 840 (6th Cir. 2002).
[15] *Trans World Airlines, Inc. v. Thurston*, 469 U.S. 111, 126 (1985).
[16] *Id.*, 128-129.
[17] *Id.*.

'Willful' does not have the same meaning as 'intentional' in ADEA cases.

The Court narrowed the range of cases where willfulness could be found in 1988 when it issued a divided 6-to-3 opinion that involved a violation of the Fair Labor Standards Act.[18] Justice John Paul Stevens wrote that even an unreasonable action by an employer does not constitute willfulness if it is not reckless. Justice Stevens said the word "willful" refers to conduct that is not merely negligent but is "voluntary," "deliberate," or "intentional."

Then, the Court ruled *Hazen Paper Co. v. Biggins* in 1993 that a violation is not willful if the employer acted "incorrectly but in good faith and nonrecklessly" and "believes that the statute permits a particular age-based decision..."[19] Justice Sandra Day O'Connor reasoned that the ADEA is unique among civil rights law because it is not an "unqualified prohibition" on the use of age in employment decision.[20]

The Court said it is not willful if the employer acted in good faith and was not reckless.

Given these rulings, a finding of willfulness may be denied even unless it can be shown the employer acted with

---

[18] *McLaughlin v. Richland Shoe Co.*, 486 U.S. 128 (1988).
[19] *Hazen Paper Co. v. Biggins*, 507 U.S. 604, 616 (1993).
[20] *Id.*

reckless disregard or with deliberate indifference to the employer's legal duty under the ADEA.

An appellate court in 1995 found willful age discrimination in a case where a top supervisor ordered a first-line supervisor to doctor an employee's performance appraisals to show poor performance to justify the employee's subsequent lay-off. The court said the jury could conclude that the employer knew or showed reckless disregard for the ADEA.[21]

A federal judge in Connecticut upheld a finding of willfulness in a 2000 case involving a reduction in force by United Technologies Corp.[22] The employer used a "highly unusual process" to select workers for layoff that employed no written instructions or criterion and lacked any documentation. "At the least... the evidence supported a finding of 'reckless disregard'... At the most, the jury could have inferred from defendant's efforts at obliterating any paper trail, a purposeful attempt to avoid the requirements of the law by insulating the decision-making process and deflecting the responsibility from any one individual," wrote the court.[23]

---

[21] *Starceski v. Westinghouse Elec. Corp.*, 54 F.3d 1089, 1096 (3d Cir. 1995).
[22] *Schanzer v. United Technologies Corp.*, 120 F.Supp.2d 200 (D.Conn. 2000).
[23] *Schanzer*, 120 F. Supp. 2nd. at 212.

In a 2002 case, a federal appeals court upheld a jury's finding of willfulness where an employer destroyed records related to a reduction-in-force in violation of the company's own record-keeping policy.[24]

➢ Prejudgment Interest

The U.S. Supreme Court ruled in a 1988 case that there is a strong presumption that prejudgment interest on back-pay awards should be granted in employment discrimination cases.[25] The U.S. Court of Appeals for the Second Circuit in New York takes the position that it is an abuse of judicial discretion to deny prejudgment interest on lost wages in an ADEA case.[26]

Many federal circuits, however, do not award prejudgment interest on an award of liquidated damages for willful age discrimination.[27] These courts hold that prejudgment interest, on top of liquidated damages, constitutes a "double recovery."[28] They note the Fair Labor Standards Act, upon which the ADEA damages formula is

---

[24] *Tyler v. Union Oil Co. of Cal.*, 304 F.3d 379 (5th Cir. 2002).
[25] *Loeffler v. Frank*, 486 U.S. 549, 557-58 (1988).
[26] *Sharkey v. Lasmo*, 214 F.3d 371, 375 (2nd Cir. 2000).
[27] *See* , e.g. *Miller v. Raytheon Co.*, 716 F.3d (5th Cir. 2013).
[28] *Lindsey v. American Case Iron Pipe Co*, 8g10 F.2d 1094 (11th Cir. 1987).

patterned, does not permit both an award of prejudgment interest and liquidated damages.[29]

Plaintiffs are expected to specifically request pre-judgment interest. One appellate court has ruled that prejudgment interest is barred in an ADEA action where the prevailing plaintiff did not file a motion to alter or amend the judgment within 10 days as is required by Fed. R. Civ. P. 59(e).[30]

➢ Attorney fees & Costs

Without the promise of attorney fees, most age discrimination cases would never be litigated. The majority of ADEA cases involve job loss, which leaves the victim without income. Unlike attorneys who represent employers, attorneys who represent discrimination victims often work independently or in small firms and cannot afford to subsidize years of work without the assurance of compensation down the road.

Courts must award reasonable attorney fees to prevailing plaintiffs.

---

[29] *See* i.e., *Lindsey v. American Cast Iron Pipe Co.*, 810 F.2d 1094 (11th Cir. 1987)(holding prejudgment interest is available for liquidated damages) and *Powers v. Grinnell Corp.*, 915 F.2d 34 (1st Cir. 1990)(holding prejudgment interest may not be awarded if liquidated damages are awarded under the ADEA).
[30] *Goodman v. Heublein, Inc.*, 682 F.2d 44, 45 (2d Cir. 1982).

Fortunately, the ADEA requires a district court to award reasonable attorney fees to a plaintiff who is a prevailing party. The ADEA has a more favorable attorneys fee provision than Title VII of the Civil Rights Act, which says the court "may" award reasonable attorney fees. Specifically, the FLSA, and consequently the ADEA, provides that the "court in such action shall, in addition to any judgment awarded to the plaintiff or plaintiffs, allow a reasonable attorney's fee to be paid by the defendant." [31]

There are rare circumstances where attorney fees can be denied to a prevailing plaintiff in an age discrimination case. A "prevailing party" is one who succeeds in winning a judgment on a "significant issue" and obtaining relief that "materially alters the legal relationship between the parties."[32] The ADEA provides only for monetary damages. Courts have held that ADEA plaintiffs who cannot show they suffered any monetary damages technically are not prevailing plaintiffs because they are not entitled to any relief.

Damaged but Not Entitled to Damages

John, 62, had worked as a manager at a manufacturing company for two decades. Shortly

---

[31] 29 U.S.C. § 216(b).
[32] *Farrar v. Hobby*, 506 U.S. 103, 104 (1992).

after it was purchased by a large corporation, John's new supervisor summoned him into his office.

"Sorry John," said the boss, "We've got to let you go. It doesn't make sense to train a manager who will probably retire in a year or two."

No sooner did John get home than his phone rang. It was the chief executive officer of a competing manufacturing company. She heard that John was fired and asked him to head up a new division at a higher salary than he formerly earned. John accepted the position.

After hanging up, John called his attorney and said he wanted to sue his former employer for age discrimination. His attorney advised against it.

The ADEA reimburses age discrimination plaintiffs for monetary loss only. Since John already had a new and better paying job, he would not suffer monetary loss. Therefore, John likely would not be eligible for damages in an ADEA lawsuit.

John wanted to sue anyway because he was so outraged about his callous and discriminatory treatment.

The attorney said John would not be considered a prevailing party in the lawsuit because he had no damages, and therefore John could be held responsible for paying his attorney fees and courts costs out of his own pocket.

John decided not to sue.

♦

Plaintiffs generally "prevail" only when the court issues a judgment or enforces a settlement through a consent decree. Attorney fees may not be available, for example, if the plaintiff agrees to a settlement where the court did not retain jurisdiction or provide any indication of approval or disapproval of the settlement.

A prevailing party also is entitled to recover costs, including court fees and printing costs, pursuant to the Federal Rule of Civil Procedure 54(d).

➢ Taxes

The U.S. Supreme Court has ruled that an award of back pay, front pay and liquidated damages under the ADEA is not excludible from a taxpayer's gross income.[33] This income is taxable as wages. Some federal appellate courts have ruled that employers should withhold payroll taxes from an award of back pay or front pay.[34]

---

[33] *Commissioner v. Schleier*, 115 S.Ct. 2159 (1995).
[34] *See Cifuentes v. Costco Wholesale Corporation*, Cal. Court of Appeal, 2nd Appellate District (June 26, 2015).

The Court notes in *Commissioner v. Schleirer* that IRS regulations exclude damages from income when a judgment or settlement is derived from physical injuries or sickness. The Court acknowledged that unlawful termination in violation of the ADEA may cause "some psychological or personal injury comparable to the intangible pain and suffering caused by an automobile accident." However, the Court said liquidated damages under the ADEA are meant to be "punitive in nature; thus, they serve no compensatory function and cannot be described as being 'on account of personal injuries.'"

Plaintiffs can ask a court to order an employer to pay taxes due on a lump sum payment of back wages.

One saving grace for age discrimination victims is that the court may order the defendant to compensate the plaintiff for taxes stemming from a lump sum award of back pay. The plaintiff must demonstrate the amount of the income tax burden that is the basis for the award.[35]

An Administrative Law Judge ruled in *Smets v. Department of the Navy*, EEOC Appeal No. 01A45224 (July 19, 2005), that the complainant was a victim of age discrimination when she

---

[35] *Barbour v. Medlantic Mgmt. Corp.*, 952 F. Supp. 857, 865 (D.D.C. 1997) (denying award due to plaintiff's failure to provide evidence on difference between taxes paid on lump sum front pay award and amount of taxes that would have been paid had the salary been earned over time).

was not selected for a position. The judge ordered the defendant to compensate the plaintiff for the increased tax liability resulting from a lump-sum payment.

➤ Settlement

An employer has an incentive to negotiate a settlement if a case survives a motion for summary judgment because of the financial risk posed by a jury trial. According to a study funded by the American Bar Foundation (ABF), about half of all employment discrimination cases end in a settlement (athough the number is thought to be smaller for age discrimination cases).[36]

Slightly over 40 percent of plaintiffs interviewed by the ABF said they had hoped to get their jobs back or, if they were still employed when they filed the ADEA lawsuit, to keep their jobs. The ABF study found that this almost never happens.

> *It is wise to have realistic expectations regarding a settlement to avoid disappointment.*

Sam Grayson, a white police officer, is quoted by the ABF as stating the $100,000 settlement of his discrimination case is "not anything big." He said a large portion went to his

---

[36])*See* Neilsen, Laura B., et al., *Individual Justice or Collective Legal Mobilization? Employment Discrimination Litigation in the Post-Civil Rights United States*, 7 Journal of Empirical Legal Studies 2, 175-201 (June 2010).

attorney. "I didn't want any money. I wanted my job back... [T]o be completely honest with you, [I] cried and... felt like I lost because it wasn't about the money," he said.

An employment attorney who represents employers told ABF researchers: "[T]he majority of our cases will either settle early for nuisance value or lower values where we can at least make the business case that it's going to cost us less to enter into the settlement than it would be to proceed." When pressed to define nuisance value, the attorney said, "Maybe $1,000 or $1,500 or something."

In its 2014 performance report, the EEOC states that its mediation program for private sector complainants that year achieved a settlement in 7,846 cases representing all types of discrimination.

Mediation is a voluntary process where a neutral mediator assists the employer and employee in reaching an early and confidential resolution of the employment dispute raised in a charge of discrimination.

The EEOC states its mediation program yielded $144.6 million in monetary benefits for complainants in 2014.

Simple division indicates the EEOC's mediation effort yielded about $18,430 per mediation. Given that most age discrimination charges are filed by workers who lost their jobs, a settlement of less than $20,000 would not come close to restoring them to the position they occupied prior to the discrimination.

20. FINAL THOUGHTS

Society turns away from the aged worker as though he belonged to another species - *Simone de Beauvoir*, THE COMING OF AGE (1970).

There has been a revolution in America since the adoption of the ADEA. We have seen the advent of computer technology, robots that replace human beings on assembly lines and the astounding rise of the Internet. But one thing has not changed significantly - the ADEA.

For a half century, older workers have been treated like second-class citizens under U.S. law and by all three branches of federal government. Society's attitudes have evolved with respect employment discrimination on the basis of race, sex, religion, national origin and disability. But not age discrimination. This is a reflection of how deeply entrenched and systemic the problem of ageism is in our society. But it is far more than that.

Age discrimination is not a victimless crime. It is a devastating blow to loyal and hard-working Americans, most of whom who followed the rules all their lives. It evokes a sense of deep betrayal, outrage, cynicism and depression. But the problem goes far deeper even than this.

Older workers often suffer an array of health impacts when they are unfairly terminated from a job that is at the core of their well-being. Being the victim of age discrimination can open a Pandora's Box of mental and physical ills, from anxiety and depression to substance abuse and suicide. Victims of age discrimination often are dumped into chronic unemployment. Research shows that many jobless older workers forgo routine health care because of lack of funds or the need to pay other bills.

> *For millions of Americans, the cost of age discrimination is an old age without dignity.*

Worse, age discrimination consigns millions of older workers to poverty or near poverty for the rest of their lives. The Economic Policy Institute in 2013 estimated that almost half of Americans aged 65 and older live in poverty or near poverty. Many age discrimination victims, especially women and minorities, are reduced to relying upon food banks after a lifetime of hard work. They are forced to choose between going to the dentist or buying a hearing aid. They pinch pennies for things that younger Americans take for granted – like joining friends at a movie matinee or for an early-bird dinner at a chain restaurant.

Whose fault is it that twenty million older Americans are in this sorry financial state? Many lost homes and savings in the appalling Wall Street rip-off that precipitated a worldwide financial collapse in 2008. The U.S. Congress sat by silently while corporations dropped employer-funded pensions, once a mainstay of retirement, in favor of employee-funded savings plans. Some would argue the lion's share of fault lies with the federal government, which collected taxes from older workers year after year throughout their working lives, with the understanding that they would be protected from Wall Street speculators and greedy corporate predators.

> *Can society really blame older workers for failing to prepare for retirement when the federal government's failure was so massive and far-reaching?*

Older workers today experience age discrimination on a scale never before seen. Employers and staffing agencies are using the internet and computer software programs to screen out the resumes of older workers. The national media has covered the refusal of some of America's largest corporations, including Google and Microsoft, to hire older workers. But nothing is done to curtail this abuse! Meanwhile, corporations manipulate loopholes in the ADEA and exploit pro-business federal court rulings to replace older workers with cheaper younger workers in bogus "restructurings" and "downsizings."

There is simply NO legal or moral justification for treating age discrimination differently than race or sex discrimination. If older workers can't do the job, they should be subject to the same rules, policies and practices that every other worker is subject to. No more and no less.

Yet, older workers are forced to compete in a kind of Darwinian "survival of the fittest" struggle that favors the brute strength of youth. As they age, workers are confronted with a creeping tide of ageism and bias by employers in search of higher profits. They must increasingly battle to retain their basic human right to be treated with dignity and respect. Finally, they must fight to even remain in the workforce so they can support themselves and their families, save for retirement and stave off poverty.

If this sounds unfair, contact your representatives in the U.S. Congress and demand change.

Tell them age discrimination is no different than any other kind of employment discrimination and should be treated with the same severity.

I have urged Congress to repeal the ADEA and to add age as a protected class to Title VII of the Civil Rights Act of 1964. Older workers are entitled at least to the same rights as other protected classes. Then we must all demand that the

U.S. Supreme Court and our federal courts treat employment discrimination seriously. These cases are not pesky distractions from more weighty matters. Equality and equal justice were of paramount importance to America's founders in 1776 and are no less vital today! I have urged the creation of a specialized federal appeals court (akin to bankruptcy and tax courts) dedicated to employment discrimination cases.

President Barack H. Obama is leaving office and, hopefully, the new President will repeal Obama's misguided 2010 executive order that permits the federal government to discriminate against older workers.

Finally, older Americans need advocacy in the media, the court system and the halls of Congress. Why is there so little understanding or outrage about the way that age discrimination is ignored, tolerated and treated as a lesser offense under the law? Where is the National Organization for Women or the NAACP for older workers? Surely, the very architects of the civil rights movement will not accede to a devastating civil rights violation with nary a whimper.

Older workers must demand our right to equal justice under the law.

Appendix

➢ EEOC Office List

EEOC HEADQUARTERS:

U.S. Equal Employment Opportunity Commission
131 M Street, NE
Washington, DC 20507
202-663-4900 / (TTY) 202-663-4494

ALABAMA

- **EEOC Birmingham District Office**
  Ridge Park Place
  1130 22nd Street South
  Suite 2000
  Birmingham, AL 35205
  Phone: 1-800-669-4000
- **EEOC Mobile Local Office**
  63 South Royal Street
  Suite 504
  Mobile, AL 36602
  Phone: 1-800-669-4000

ARKANSAS

- **EEOC Little Rock Area Office**
  820 Louisiana Street
  Suite 200
  Little Rock, Arkansas 72201
  Phone: 1-800-669-4000

ARIZONA

- **EEOC Phoenix District Office**
  3300 North Central Avenue
  Suite 690
  Phoenix, AZ 85012-2504
  Phone: 1-800-669-4000

CALIFORNIA

- **EEOC Los Angeles District Office**
  Roybal Federal Building
  255 East Temple St., 4th Floor
  Los Angeles, CA 90012
  Phone: 1-800-669-4000
- **EEOC Fresno Local Office**
  2300 Tulare Street
  Suite 215
  Fresno, CA 93721
  Phone: 1-800-669-4000
- **EEOC San Diego Local Office**
  555 West Beech Street,
  Suite 504,
  San Diego, CA 92101
  Phone: 1-800-669-4000
- **EEOC San Francisco District Office**
  450 Golden Gate Avenue
  5 West, P.O Box 36025
  San Francisco, CA 94102-3661
  Phone: 1-800-669-4000
- **EEOC Oakland Local Office**
  1301 Clay Street
  Suite 1170-N
  Oakland, CA 94612-5217
  Phone: 1-800-669-4000
- **EEOC San Jose Local Office**
  96 N. Third St., Suite 250
  San Jose, CA 95112
  Phone: 1-800-669-4000

COLORADO

- **EEOC Denver Field Office**
  303 E. 17th Avenue
  Suite 410
  Denver, Colorado 80203
  Phone: 1-800-669-4000

DISTRICT OF COLUMBIA

- **EEOC Washington DC Field Office**
  131 M Street, NE
  Fourth Floor, Suite 4NWO2F
  Washington, DC 20507-0100
  Phone: 1-800-669-4000

FLORIDA

- **EEOC Miami District Office**
  Miami Tower
  100 SE 2nd Street, Suite 1500
  Miami FL 33131
  Phone: 1-800-669-4000
- **EEOC Tampa Field Office**
  501 East Polk Street, Suite 1000
  Tampa, FL 33602
  Phone: 1-800-669-4000

GEORGIA

- **EEOC Atlanta District Office**
  Sam Nunn Atlanta Federal Center
  100 Alabama Street, SW, Suite 4R30
  Atlanta, Georgia 30303
  Phone: 1-800-669-4000
- **EEOC Savannah Local Office**
  7391 Hodgson Memorial Drive, Suite 200
  Savannah, GA 31406-2579
  Phone: 1-800-669-4000

HAWAII

- **EEOC Honolulu Local Office**
  300 Ala Moana Blvd
  Room 7-127
  P.O. Box 50082
  Honolulu, HI 96850-0051
  Phone: 1-800-669-4000

ILLINOIS

- **EEOC Chicago District Office**
  500 West Madison Street
  Suite 2000
  Chicago, Illinois 60661
  Phone: 1-800-669-4000

INDIANA

- **EEOC Indianapolis Office**
  101 West Ohio St, Suite 1900
  Indianapolis, IN 46204
  Phone: 1-800-669-4000

KANSAS

- **EEOC Kansas City Area Office**
  Gateway Tower II
  400 State Ave., Suite 905
  Kansas City, KS 66101
  Phone: 1-800-669-4000

KENTUCY

- **EEOC Louisville Area Office**
  600 Dr. Martin Luther King, Jr. Place
  Suite 268
  Louisville, Kentucky 40202
  Phone: 1-800-669-4000

LOUISIANA

- **EEOC New Orleans Field Office**
  Hale Boggs Federal Building
  500 Poydras Street, Suite 800
  New Orleans, LA 70113
  Phone: 1-800-669-4000

MARYLAND

- **EEOC Baltimore Field Office**
  City Crescent Building
  10 S. Howard Street
  Third Floor

Baltimore, MD 21201
Phone: 1-800-669-4000.

MASSACHUSETTS

- **EEOC Boston Area Office**
  John F. Kennedy Federal Building
  475 Government Center
  Boston, MA 02203
  Phone: 1-800-669-4000

MICHIGAN

- **EEOC Detroit Field Office**
  Patrick V. McNamara Building
  477 Michigan Avenue
  Room 865
  Detroit, MI 48226
  Phone: 1-800-669-4000

MINNESOTA

- **EEOC Minneapolis Area Office**
  Towle Building
  330 South Second Avenue, Suite 720
  Minneapolis, MN 55401-2224
  Phone: 1-800-669-4000

MISSISSIPPI

- **EEOC Jackson Area Office**
  Dr. A. H. McCoy Federal Building
  100 West Capitol Street, Suite 338
  Jackson, Mississippi 39269
  Phone: 1-800-669-4000

MISSOURI

- **EEOC St. Louis District Office**
  Robert A. Young Federal Building
  1222 Spruce St.
  Rm 8.100
  St. Louis, MO 63103
  Phone: 1-800-669-4000

NEVADA

- **EEOC Las Vegas Local Office**
  333 Las Vegas Blvd South
  Suite 8112
  Las Vegas, NV 89101
  Phone: 1-800-669-4000

NEW MEXICO

- **EEOC Albuquerque Area Office**
  505 Marquette Avenue, NW
  Suite 900 - 9th Floor
  Albuquerque, NM 87102
  Phone: 1-800-669-4000

NEW JERSEY

- **EEOC Newark Area Office**
  Two Gateway Center
  Suite 1703
  283-299 Market Street
  Newark, NJ 07102
  Phone: 1-800-669-4000

NEW YORK

- **EEOC New York District Office**
  33 Whitehall Street, 5th Floor
  New York, NY 10004
  Phone: 1-800-669-4000
- **EEOC Buffalo Local Office**
  6 Fountain Plaza
  Suite 350
  Buffalo, NY 14202
  Phone: 1-800-669-4000

NORTH CAROLINA

- **EEOC Charlotte District Office**
  129 West Trade Street
  Suite 400
  Charlotte, North Carolina 28202
  Phone: 1-800-669-4000
- **EEOC Raleigh Area Office**
  434 Fayetteville Street, Suite 700
  Raleigh, NC 27601-1701

Phone: 1-800-669-4000

- **EEOC Greensboro Local Office**
  Suite 201
  2303 W. Meadowview Road
  Greensboro, N.C. 27407
  Phone: 1-800-669-4000
- **EEOC Greenville Local Office**
  Suite 201
  2303 W. Meadowview Road
  Greensboro, N.C. 27407
  Phone: 1-800-669-4000

OHIO

- **EEOC Cincinnati Area Office**
  John W. Peck Federal
  Office Building
  550 Main Street, 10th
  Floor
  Cincinnati, OH 45202
  Phone: 1-800-669-4000
- **EEOC Cleveland Field Office**
  Anthony J. Celebrezze
  Federal Building
  1240 E. 9th Street, Suite
  3001
  Cleveland, OH 44199
  Phone: 1-800-669-4000.

OKLAHOMA

- **EEOC Oklahoma City Area Office**
  215 Dean A McGee
  Avenue
  Suite 524
  Oklahoma City, Oklahoma
  73102
  Phone: 1-800-669-4000

PENNSYLVANIA

- **EEOC Philadelphia District Office**
  801 Market Street, Suite
  1300
  Philadelphia, PA 19107-
  3127
  Phone: For general
  inquiries or to begin the
  process of filing a
  complaint of

discrimination, call 1-800-
669-4000.

- **EEOC Pittsburgh Area Office**
  William S. Moorhead
  Federal Building
  1000 Liberty Avenue, Suite
  1112
  Pittsburgh, PA 15222
  Phone:1-800-669-4000.

TENNESSEE

- **EEOC Memphis District Office**
  1407 Union Avenue, 9th
  floor
  Memphis, TN 38104
  Phone: 1-800-669-4000
- **EEOC Nashville Area Office**
  220 Athens Way
  Suite 350
  Nashville, TN 37228-9940
  Phone: 1-800-669-4000.

TEXAS

- **EEOC Dallas District Office**
  207 S. Houston Street
  3rd Floor
  Dallas, Texas 75202
  Phone: 1-800-669-4000
- **EEOC San Antonio Field Office**
  Legacy Oaks, Building A
  5410 Fredericksburg Road
  Suite 200
  San Antonio, TX 78229
  Phone: 1-800-669-4000
- **EEOC El Paso Area Office**
  300 E. Main Dr.
  Suite 500
  El Paso, Texas 79901
  Phone: 1-800-669-4000
- **EEOC Houston District Office**
  Mickey Leland Building
  1919 Smith Street
  7th Floor
  Houston, Texas 77002
  Phone: 1-800-669-4000

VIRGINIA

- **EEOC Norfolk Local Office**
  Federal Building
  200 Granby Street
  Suite 739
  Norfolk, VA 23510
  Phone: 1-800-669-4000
- **EEOC Richmond Local Office**
  400 N. Eight Street
  Suite 350
  Richmond, VA 23219
  Phone: 1-800-669-4000

WASHINGTON

- **EEOC Seattle Field Office**
  Federal Office Building
  909 First Avenue
  Suite 400
  Seattle, WA 98104-1061
  Phone: 1-800-669-4000

WISCONSIN

- **EEOC Milwaukee Area Office**
  Reuss Federal Plaza
  310 West Wisconsin
  Avenue, Suite 500
  Milwaukee, WI 53203-2292
  Phone: 1-800-669-4000

PUERTO RICO

- **EEOC San Juan Local Office**
  525 F.D. Roosevelt Ave.
  Plaza Las Americas, Suite 1202
  San Juan, Puerto Rico
  00918-8001
  Phone: 1-800-669-4000

➢ Federal Agencies & Employee Benefits

- **Department of Labor (DOL)**

  The Pension and Welfare Benefits Administration of the Department of Labor (DOL) enforces the provisions of the Employee Retirement Income Security Act (ERISA) that deal with the operation of pension plans, the preservation of plan assets, and the proper disposition of plan assets. DOL ascertains that employers are investing and safeguarding plan assets for the benefit of the employees, not the employer.

- **Internal Revenue Service (IRS)**

  The Employee Plans Division of the Internal Revenue Service enforces the tax aspects of employee benefit plans, with special emphasis on the legality of pension plans. To encourage employers and employees to save actively to pay for the employees' retirement, employers that maintain pension plans are permitted favorable tax treatment for their contributions to the plans, including tax deductions and delayed taxation for plan earnings. The Internal Revenue Code sets out detailed rules for determining whether or not a pension plan qualifies for favorable tax treatment.

- **Pension Benefit Guaranty Trust Corp. (PBGC)**

  PBGC provides insurance to guarantee the pensions of plan participants in the event that plan assets are inadequate to cover employees' pensions

INDEX

Printed in Great Britain
by Amazon